This Book

presented to the

CHURCH LIBRARY IN MEMORY OF

Mr. Lloyd W. Gunn
(brother of Faye Dillard)

BY

Mr. & Mrs. H. A. McBee

Code 436-373, No. 3, Broadman Supplies, Nashville, Tenn. Printed in USA

**WHEN
GOD MADE
<u>YOU</u>,
HE
KNEW WHAT
HE WAS DOING**

By James W. Angell

Put Your Arms Around the City
When God Made *You*, He Knew What He Was Doing

WHEN GOD MADE YOU, HE KNEW WHAT HE WAS DOING

James W. Angell

Fleming H. Revell Company
Old Tappan, New Jersey

ISBN 0–8007–0486–X
Copyright © 1972 by Fleming H. Revell Company
All Rights Reserved
Library of Congress Catalog Card Number: 70–172687
Printed in the United States of America

TO our children:
Ann, Susan, Jim, and Mary Scott
whose lives confirm, better than words,
a Divine premeditation.

Acknowledgments

Grateful acknowledgment is made for the use of copyrighted material.

Scripture quotations identified as RSV are from the *Revised Standard Version of the Bible,* copyrighted 1946 and 1952.

Scripture quotations identified as KJV are from the *King James Version of the Bible.*

Scripture quotations identified as NEB are from *The New English Bible,* © the Delegates of the Oxford University Press and the Syndics of the Cambridge University Press, 1961. Reprinted by permission.

Poem by Frank Whitney, "I Behold the Christ in You," reprinted by permission of *Unity.*

Prayer "Our day is..." from the book *The Temple* by W.E. Orchard. Copyright 1918 by E.P. Dutton & Co., Inc. Renewal 1946 by W.E. Orchard. Published by E.P. Dutton & Co., Inc., and reprinted with their permission.

Poem from *Please Touch* by Edwin M. McMahon and Peter A. Campbell © Sheed and Ward Inc., 1969.

Poem "We Are Transmitters-" by D.H. Lawrence from *The Complete Poems* of D.H. Lawrence, Volume I, edited by Vivian de Sola Pinto and F. Warren Roberts and The Viking Press, Inc.

Quotation from John Killinger's book *For God's Sake, Be Human,* published by Word Books, copyright 1970.

Poem "Hold April" from *Hold April* by Jesse Stuart. Copyright © 1962 by Jesse Stuart. Used with permission of McGraw-Hill Book Company.

Quotation by Nikos Kazantzakis from *Zorba the Greek,* copyright © 1952 by Simon & Schuster. Used with permission of Simon & Schuster, Inc.

Song, "Little Boxes," words and music by Malvina Reynolds © copyright 1962 by Schroder Music Co. (ASCAP). Used by permission.

The selection "Time" is from *Time for All Things* by Charlie W. Shedd. Copyright © 1962 by Abingdon Press. Used by permission.

Selection by Christopher Fry from *A Sleep of Prisoners,* published by Oxford University Press. Used by permission.

Words from the Fred Waring choral edition *Open Your Heart To Spring,* words by Harriet Moore, music by Marian Chaplin. © Copyright MCMLVI, Shawnee Press, Inc., Delaware Water Gap, Pa.

The selection from *The Crucible of Redemption* by Carlyle Marney is copyrighted © 1968 by Abingdon Press and used by permission.

The poem by William Carlos Williams is from *Pictures From Brueghel and Other Poems.* Copyright 1954 by William Carlos Williams. Reprinted by permission of New Directions Publishing Corporation.

"Richard Cory" is reprinted by permission of Charles Scribner's Sons from *The Children of the Night* by Edwin Arlington Robinson (1897).

"If There Is a Holy Spirit" by Richard Avery and Donald Marsh is from HYMNS HOT AND CAROLS COOL © 1967 by Proclamation Productions, Inc. Port Jervis, N.Y. Used by permission.

The selection from *I Saw God Wash the World* is copyrighted by William L. Stidger; The Rodeheaver Co., Agent. Used by permission.

The selection from *Credo* by Thomas S. Kepler is reprinted from *motive,* 1944. Copyright © 1944 by the Board of Education of the Methodist Church. Used by permission of the publishers.

The selection from *The Celebration of Flesh* by Arthur C. McGill. Copyrighted © 1964 by Association Press, N. Y., N. Y. Used by permission.

Lines taken from *Fiddler on the Roof* by Joseph Stein copyright © 1964 by Joseph Stein. Music and lyrics copyright © 1964 by Sunbeam Music Corporation. Used by permission of Crown Publishers, Inc.

The lines from a sermon by Liston Pope in *Preaching the Resurrection,* edited by Alton M. Motter, © 1959, are used by permission of Fortress Press.

The selection from "The Bird and the Machine," copyright © 1955 by Loren Eiseley, is reprinted from THE IMMENSE JOURNEY by Loren Eiseley by permission of Random House, Inc.

"The Excesses of God" by Robinson Jeffers, copyright 1941 and renewed 1969 by Donnan Jeffers and Garth Jeffers, is reprinted from SELECTED POEMS by Robinson Jeffers, by permission of Random House, Inc.

FIRST BAPTIST CHURCH LIBRARY
TOMBALL, TEXAS

Contents

	INTRODUCTION	
I	HEY, I'M NOT SO BAD!	
	1. There Is Only One You. Is That Good News or Bad?	17
	2. I See the Beginning of Eloquence	23
	3. Believing Is Touching	28
	4. The Sacrament of Yourself	33
II	TOMORROW JUST GOT HERE	
	5. How We Misspelled SUCCES by Really Trying	43
	6. Persons Versus Purple Cows: I'd Rather Be Than See One	49
	7. Has God Changed His Mind About Sex?	54
	8. America Is Still Being Born	63
III	I WONDER AS I WANDER	
	9. And to Think We Found You in the Yellow Pages!	71
	10. Let's Dress Up and Play Life	76
	11. The Hidden Person	81
	12. If There Is a Holy Spirit—	90
IV	HE AIN'T HEAVY FATHER; HE'S MY BROTHER	
	13. Theodore Hesburgh Skins Our Eyes	99
	14. Martin Luther King, Jr., and	

	Robert Kennedy Return to Ask Some Questions	106
	15. Whatever Is Necessary to Get My People Out of Hell	110
	16. Moonrocks Are Valuable, But So Are People	117
V	A PIECE OF THE ACTION	
	17. The Truth Is Something You Do	125
	18. Jonah Was a Cop-out	128
	19. If You Were Arrested for Being a Christian, How Much Evidence Would There Be Against You?	134
	20. How Do You Feel When People Ask You What You Do for a Living?	140
VI	IS NECESSARY FOR PEACE	
	21. Make Peace With Yesterday	149
	22. Peace Is a Journey	154
	23. Prayer Creates a New Situation	159
	24. Four Feet From Death	166
VII	TODAY IS THE BEST CHANCE YOU'LL EVER HAVE	
	25. I'm Telling You Kids for the Last Time!	173
	26. On a Clear Day You Can See Forever	177
	27. When We're Crying We Know We're Not Dead	183
	28. Open Your Heart to Spring	187

Introduction

My friend Dr. Edwin Aymes is a Los Angeles neurosurgeon and, incidentally, a fine theologian. I have learned much from him. Certain things I have heard him say about the treatment of patients have helped me clarify my role as a hawker of the good news of Christianity.

One day he remarked, "The biggest trouble my patients have is that they are unable to love themselves. And I mean the majority of them!"

This book is concerned with Christian techniques of feeling good about yourself, with probing contemporary meanings of what Jesus implied when he said, "You shall love . . . your neighbor as yourself" (Luke 10:27 RSV). To achieve this is not to reject the church's teaching about sin. It is, rather, to find the secret of freedom.

There are scads of self-help books on the market. What I have tried to do is different from most of them in the respect that it isn't neutral concerning the God who is proclaimed in the Judeo-Christian tradition. It aggressively draws the Spirit of God, the church, Jesus of Nazareth, the Bible, and the "tools of faith" into the discussion of self-worth. It works them into what, hopefully, will be practical suggestions for racing recklessly past self-acceptance to self-affirmation in the same way those barrier-smashing drivers do in a TV oil company commercial.

This is a subject the church needs to deal with. Until we get "unhung-up" at this point, all other data on the new life sounds academic and far away.

Social workers, with whom I have discussed the attitudes people have about themselves, refer to self-esteem, self-confidence, wholesome self-love as Rule One. And, as you will see, the personal and social dimensions are intertangled.

My high-school-age son, Jim, brought home an English theme one day. Beside one especially good paragraph, his teacher had noted in the margin, "I see the beginning of eloquence." Afterwards, I detected a fresh light in his eyes and a springier spring in his step. This happens to all of us when other persons recognize in us exciting raw material. It is a universal key that turns a universal lock.

JAMES W. ANGELL

I
HEY, I'M NOT SO BAD!

1
There Is Only One You. Is That Good News or Bad?

> The lack of self-esteem is one of the commonest problems in the world today and the problem behind most of the troubles people get into.
>
> —JEAN MURPHY

There is only one you. And that's good news. People are snowflakes: no two are alike. Each of us is a special design and combination of mystic material. Anyone who has ever been in love—like halfway out of his skull—knows there isn't a truer statement on Earth.

This book is about believing in yourself as a way of becoming yourself.

In *You're a Good Man, Charlie Brown* Charlie sings, "I'm awful glad I'm me!" I want to turn you into Charlie Brown.

Some years ago *Life* magazine featured on its cover a happy youngster astride a pony. The caption was "On Her Pony Macaroni: The Fun of Being Caroline Kennedy." I want you to become Caroline.

Better still, to become *you*.

At times, each of us has trouble living with himself. And most of us, most of the time, underestimate the excitement there is in really being ourselves.

Maury Wills, star player on the Los Angeles Dodgers baseball team, was being questioned one night after a game about an especially impressive performance. He tried to explain why he had been successful in "putting it all together."

"Here's what it is," he said. "I am being myself and nothing more. In Montreal I felt I had to do more, but by doing more, I did less."

This book will argue: If you will dare to look at yourself through God's eyes, you will recognize someone whose life has amazing potential. You will begin to believe you are a greater invention than Kleenex. When God made *you,* He knew what He was doing.

Finding our identity isn't easy. John Keats called it an "adventurous problem." To know yourself is like being asked to explain the universe and its surroundings. The prodigal son was far down the highway of experience before he "came to himself."

If you are stymied or have decided the "real you" is lost somewhere in the strange forests of mass conformity, read on and take heart.

Begin with this: The journey could be fun.

The word *fun* doesn't appear in the Bible, but it belongs in the vocabulary of every whole person.

Jesus is not often associated with fun, nor do the gospels make reference to His laughter. But it's between the lines. His eyes sparkled as often as His words. Elton Trueblood found enough humor in His ministry to write an entire book about it. The Man of sorrows comes more easily to our minds, but I like to see Him handling a spirited horse at age sixteen, taking an enthusiastic part in competitive games, or exploding in a burst of joy at some antic of Peter. How could we omit that kind of humanness from any believable portrait of True Man?

> My Master was a Man, who knew
> The rush of rain, the drip of dew,
> The wistful whisper of the breeze,
> Night's magic and its mysteries.
>
> His feet were stained by dusty ways,
> His cheeks were brown as autumn days;

> His skin it had the look of one
> Who knew the blazing balm of sun.
>
> He walked alone upon the sea,
> Spoke peace to wave-washed Galilee;
> All shores and seas were in His thought,
> This Man, god-bred, star-led, sky taught.
>
> WILLIAM L. STIDGER

This is not to minimize suffering, which is another necessary part of our humanity.

While writing this book, I went to a remote spot for several days and worked alone, miles away from my wife and children. Eating meals in solitude, I found myself remembering those years when my father lived alone after the death of my mother—remembering a long, painful procession of silent suppers and lonesome thoughts as the evenings fell in monotonous procession.

But that memory was quickly transmuted into other flashback pictures. There was Dad again, riding his motorcar along a gracefully curving Rock Island track on an Iowa spring morning, pointing out the tricks of groundhogs to a small boy seated beside and a little behind him out of the sharp taste of the wind. That was fun!

Fun is part of God's will. There is the fun of being alive. The fun of meaning. The fun of working. Learning. Seeing. Touching. Watching other lives unfold. Turning forty. Closing in on the question: *Who am I?*

Hippie-style behavior—bizarre dress, hostility toward the Establishment, and retreat to isolated regions—reveals the size of the effort some youth feel they must make in order to keep from having their identity blocked by life-dulling acculturation. Young people born since 1945 experience resentment of a society which can't seem to stop talking about the great depression and the great war. They were not part of those events, and they do not want to be controlled by them or by the people who permitted those times to be labeled *The*

Best Years of Our Lives. They feel obligated to generate their own story, ride to the top of their own mountains, state their own issues, bear their own scars, if they are to discover their own names.

This posture makes sense to Dr. Earl A. Loomis, Jr., even if it doesn't to those who frown at rebelliousness and inexcusable ingratitude for such a comfortable legacy. In *The Self in Pilgrimage* he wrote:

> No single element of the conformist's happy society is necessarily undesirable. But taken together as the be-all and end-all of life, they can be disastrous. They cut us off from the real possibilities of living, simply because they cut us off from the quest for the unique qualities in ourselves that prove each of us to be a creature of God. We force ourselves to deny even that inner restlessness to which Augustine referred when he said, "Thou hast made us for Thyself, O Lord, and our heart is restless until it finds its rest in Thee."
>
> Why do we cut ourselves off from ourselves? Part of the answer, to be sure, is that what impersonal society holds out as good, looks very good indeed. Few of us would turn down a Cadillac. None of us would grumble over a free trip to Bermuda. We like a nice change of clothing, we want our families well fed. We also want the esteem of our peers. To get it, we must succeed on their terms.
>
> It is an important part of self-discovery to participate in the life of our peers, to share in their pleasures and joys, their corporate aims and ideals. But when these goals are not organically linked to the infinitely more substantial pursuit of self-discovery, they become shallow, empty, and blind. They are substitutes that lead us to much knowledge of things, but little knowledge of others and no knowledge of self.

When the fun begins to drain out is when we fall on our faces. What happens then? What is the secret of continuing to feel good toward yourself after you've found out you're not perfect?

The essence of inward freedom is realizing that your acceptance by God is the result of His generosity, not of your having made *B* on the exam. We are not our own saviours.

But we *are* entitled to love ourselves.

We must love ourselves because God loves us.

Such is the reality of faith. And we can't add to it by little bundles of deeds flung against the sky. We can't adorn Everest by adding more snow.

We find ourselves by looking into the mirror of God's love. A bronze sun edges up over the horizon the moment our minds penetrate this truth: God loves me, not because I am perfect, but because I am His own.

A neurosurgeon in Los Angeles said, "The biggest problem my patients have is loving themselves."

This isn't hard to understand. There is so much in us that is unlovely. Although the bloom of success may be upon us temporarily, time teaches us that we are not angels, that kite strings break.

We are not devils, either.

We are naked apes *and* candles of the Lord.

God doesn't turn His love on and off depending upon our performance or lack of performance. *His* love is unilateral. Final. It pursues us wherever we go.

A man from Texas, in a moving company uniform, brought a heavy chair into our living room. In a state of late-afternoon weariness, he plopped himself in it before returning to the truck for the final pieces.

"It's hard work, isn't it?" I said, trying to show some understanding of his fatigue.

"Yes."

"Do you live near here?"

I wanted to show interest in him as a person, not just as someone paid to do a job.

"My family left me two weeks ago," he said, dejectedly. "I'm alone. Work doesn't bother me. It's a relief. I just don't know . . . . Maybe I should go back to Texas."

His eyes lingered on the floor. Though he couldn't have been more than thirty-five, he sounded old and beaten. "Tom" was stitched in red over his left chest pocket.

There is only one you, Tom. I don't know why your family left an empty house—whether it was because they didn't like California or because you were a drunk or there was a quarrel and crying—but I know this: Your life matters to God. Without Him, you will never know who you are—either in Texas or in Timbuktu.

If God is for us, nothing can destroy us permanently.

If the outlook for mankind is sometimes dismal, there are also occasions for radical wonder at the contributions that can flow from one life. The chapter entitled "Martin Luther King, Jr., and Robert Kennedy Return to Ask Some Questions" is offered as evidence.

We are accepted. We are loved. This is the basis of belief in ourselves. It is the equipment we can use to accept and love others. It opens the door to self-knowledge, self-esteem.

One Monday, I went by the post office to mail some letters. There I met a woman I had seen the day before at worship. She said favorable things about my sermon, then added, in words which came out with more seriousness than she intended, "I listen. I understand. I believe. But when I get home, I'm the same old me."

We are never equal to demands of faith. But neither are we ever just that—"the same old me." Every human meeting adds or takes away in our identity-affair with life. We are continually changing each other, helping each other affirm the value of Life and our own lives.

If we can catch even a few tiny glimpses of God, self-doubt can die. Suddenly, we will not want to be anyone other than who we already are.

2
I See the Beginning of Eloquence

> The purpose of a Christian life is not to become more Christian but less so; not to become more parochial and special but less so. The purpose of a Christian life is to become all that a human being can become, to become more fully human. Man was made in the image of the Word, and through the birth, death, and resurrection of Jesus yet more wonderfully restored in that same image. The outermost bounds of that image have never been explored. We do not yet know what it is that Christians, like other men, are capable of becoming. The old cocoons must give way to fresh life in every historical epoch. We are not yet human beings, only striving to become so.
> —MICHAEL NOVAK

In the movie version of *The Shoes of the Fisherman* Oskar Werner plays a young Roman Catholic priest who is obedient to his superiors, yet filled with stubborn questions about his faith.

In one scene he is in the process of trying to gain official approval to publish certain of his ideas. They are troubling to the fathers of the church who are charged with guarding the integrity of the classical doctrines.

The young priest is finally brought before the Curia where he is cross-examined for hours. He gives a good account of himself, but several times he is forced up against the wall intellectually. He stumbles around, is unclear, even self-contradictory. He is not nearly as confident about what he believes as these lawyers who, amid the stroking of chins and church-steepling of fingers, lead him through mazes of theological argumentation. Finally, he says with unsurrendering passion, "Though I have no precise explanations to offer, I can but say that I understand the universe to be some kind of Great Becoming."

Anthropologist Teilhard de Chardin, who also was a Roman Catholic priest, agreed that evolution is still going on. In his view, the new stages of development will be in the form of man's spiritual flowering. Life came out of the sea, he wrote, and moved through stages of increasing complexity and diversification. Now, we are witnessing convergence as men of reason and compassion band together to fend off nuclear annihilation, combat hunger, disease, and illiteracy and consolidate their dreams for peace. The process of evolution is, no longer the separation of man from the jungle, but the emergence of community. Man's next major achievement will be, not interplanetary travel, but the discovery of how men can become and stay human together.

Life is a becoming, an unfinished symphony. Man is not a thing. He is a process.

Faith says: Don't stay where you are. Evolve. Don't become a pillar of salt. Don't waste the opportunity represented by where you presently are by hiding out in either a Walter Mitty world of illusion or a John Birch world of fear. Be willing to become someone you weren't before.

Two men died.

The death of one is reported in Elliot Baker's novel *A Fine Madness*. Samson Shillitoe, the rebel-poet who rages through its pages, receives a letter from Emma, a woman who'd been caring for his father, Ben, an auto mechanic-motel owner, who had measured out his life in nuts and bolts.

> Emma had taken a whole paragraph to explain that she knew where to write him [Samson] because his father gave her the address. She seemed as reluctant to get to the point as he was to find it. But there it was.
>
> *Your father passed away about two o'clock this morning.*
>
> He read the sentence over several times to crank up some emotion, but all that sputtered within him seemed wrong. There was annoyance at the *passed away*. Ben never did anything that sneaky. He'd

died. No, even that wasn't accurate. He'd finished the dying he'd been doing most of his life. . . .

He didn't suffer any toward the end.

Another saying that had become a necessity because people wanted to believe that everything inevitable was painless. They were getting their way too. Soon there'd be a shot . . . at birth that lasted a hundred years. . . . He couldn't help wishing Emma was lying, that at about two o'clock Ben had risen from his bed . . . and let out a war whoop that cracked the bell in The First Methodist Church. But he knew it hadn't happened that way.

Two men died.

The death of the other is reported in William Manchester's *The Death of a President.* John Kennedy had been shot, and the news had gotten to his brother. But Bob Kennedy did not yet know the whole tragic story. Then the phone call came with the dreadful truth. And what was his response?

"He had the most wonderful life," Kennedy said. Later that would be his wife's most vivid recollection of his response—how, in the starless night, he remembered how bright the sun had been.

Two men died.

Of one it was said, "He'd finished the dying he'd been doing most of his life." Of the other it was said, "He had the most wonderful life."

What's the difference?

The difference is between sitting in a boat wondering if it's going to storm or risking the surf of surprise.

Jesus asks us to face the world in a spirit of hope. Admittedly, life is full of contradictions. There's enough evil in the Charles Manson murders alone to rule out the possibility of God. No one has been able to prove that it pays to be honest or that a dollar bet on goodness will get you two.

"Faith is not belief in spite of evidence," wrote Kirsopp

Lake, "but life in scorn of consequence." It overcomes the world in the same way love does. You cannot win against love. Love wins against you.

Faith in God enables us to choose glory against grimness, possibilities against perversions. We recognize ourselves as moving, our lives as unfolding, ships hailing each other in half-darkness, sailing under orders, neither abandoned nor becalmed. Faith asks us to affirm life—and ourselves.

        Mr. T.
            bareheaded
                in a soiled undershirt
his hair standing out
    on all sides
        stood on his toes
heels together
    arms gracefully
        for the moment
curled above his head.
    Then he whirled about
        bounded
into the air
    and with an *entrechat*
        perfectly achieved
completed the figure.
    My mother
        taken by surprise
where she sat
    in her invalid's chair
        was left speechless.
Bravo! she cried at last
    and clapped her hands.
        The man's wife
came from the kitchen:
    What goes on here? she said.
        But the show was over.

                                  WILLIAM CARLOS WILLIAMS

John Ciardi, commenting on this poem, says the ballet leap of Mr. T. means "Whee!"

It expresses the "whee" impulse in all of us. It denotes the way we feel in those moments when we are glad to be alive, glad the sun shines and the rain falls, glad that children are born and lovers love, that workers work and grow tired, that there is sorrow and cities and laughter and sleep and banjo noise, that some men waste money buying flowers and that a man can become a fool in order to become wise—that he can make a small leap of faith up into the air "with an *entrechat* perfectly achieved" and know his manhood is a gift from God.

There will always be something or someone that conspires to kill the "whee" with a "What goes on here?" and end the show. We will always have to deal with the routine, the shock of human cruelty, the tendency of wonder to wear thin.

Jesus is Gift because His Spirit at work in us enables us to convert every experience into the stuff of growth. We hear His call to be a brother to our brother. We go to the desert with Him and do battle against temptation. We watch Him change water into wine and start to grasp the idea that life in Him, and with Him, means that every glass of water from now on—every common event—has champagne quality. We see Him involved in a transforming encounter with Zacchaeus and know we can't get mixed up with Him and stay the same either. He pitches the crooks out of the temple, and we think of crookedness that needs to be expelled from our lives. At the cross we suffer death with Him and in exchange become conquerors of death. We are swept along in an excitement of becoming.

My son, Jim, brought home an English theme one day from Palisades High School. As a marginal notation beside one of his better paragraphs, his teacher had written, "I see the beginning of eloquence." This is what we all want others to see when we pass by.

We do not understand all the dynamics, but we understand God. His universe is not a created but a *creating* universe. It is filled with the splendor of a child learning to play a violin, with fantastic demonstrations of courage, and with love that steers the stars.

3
Believing Is Touching

>Once we believe in ourselves
> We can risk
> Curiosity . . .
>   Wonder . . .
>   Spontaneous delight
>
>Or any experience
> That reveals
> The human spirit
>
>Opening up
> A way
> Of touching
>   And judging.
>   —MC MAHON & CAMPBELL

A scene in televised American politics is familiar to everyone. A candidate edges his way through a cordoned crowd at International Airport. Escorted by the Secret Service, he advances toward a waiting limousine. Hands are flying, reaching, trying to touch history at some point by touching some personality of potential power.

The New Testament has a similar picture, and the candidate is Jesus. The crowds are the same, and the people are reaching out to touch him, too.

One woman believes that, if she can but touch the clothes he is wearing, even brush them with her fingertips, she can be healed of a hemorrhage. When she makes contact, Jesus is startled. Turning, He asks, half-curtly, "Who touched me?" The touch had been alive with meaning.

Later Jesus heals a twelve-year-old child. Mark wrote that he *took her by the hand* and told her to get up. And she got up and walked.

Touching is life's supreme mode of human communication. Better than ten thousand words.

If I put my arm around your shoulders and pull you to me, it answers twenty questions. You *feel* my friendship which is better than being told about it.

People in love have to touch each other. It's a necessity.

It's especially important for children. When we take children into a gift shop that features breakable merchandise, we say over and over, "Don't touch; just look." The child knows, though, that there is something backward about such advice. His whole life, his whole education is the result of touching. Paul Engle said: "To be a child is to heighten everything you handle." The child strokes his father's face and says, "Dad, how come you have whiskers?" He feels the silky coat of a dog, the mud between his toes, leather, glass, rubber, steel, tree bark; the authority of a kiss, the caress of a bath; snow, bricks, the mystery of pain, the warmth of a sweater; the wind—he *feels* life!

To touch is to be. It is to discover life's environment, its joys, its rules.

A Japanese sculptor confounded the curators of an American art gallery where his works were being exhibited. At the base of each statue the sculptor had placed a small sign. It read: *Please touch.*

Students at the University of Nebraska, trying to deepen their understanding of persons, held a touch-in. Crippled by myths and prejudices accumulated over many generations,

Caucasians were invited to touch black skin; black students, the skin of whites.

We learn by touching.

We love by touching.

We gain emotional poise by being touched. If there is distance, fear, or embarrassment in touching, we are without the freedom God means for us to enjoy.

Obviously, touching can also get us into difficulty. We can't touch fire without getting hurt. Insincere touching also hurts.

There's a story about deceptive touching in the Old Testament. Isaac was old and blind. He had made up his mind to give his blessing, the right to succeed as the head of the family, to Esau, whom he regarded as more honest and reliable than his brother. But Jacob dressed himself in his brother's clothing and used animal skins to cover his arms and convinced the old, blinded father that he was Esau. Through this trick he gained the prize for himself. That the act was irreversible, even though the ruse became quickly known, suggests how serious the gesture was.

Most touching is full of rewards. We are more complete human beings when we have learned to feel at home with people and with all the magic surfaces of the world.

"O world, I cannot hold thee close enough!" sang Edna St. Vincent Millay.

Said Thomas to His Lord: "Let me touch your side in order that I may believe."

Please touch.

Life is made for touching—and often reaches out to touch us. We make this remark, "What you said (or did) touched me deeply." This is touching with a difference, but still touching. People reach out and touch us with their eyes. They do selfless things to show love for us, and we feel their embrace in our core.

It may not be another person at all. Just the peacefulness of clouds, the beauty of bottle-brush, or the majesty of stars. We see something, hear something. It is Life reaching out to touch us with one of its infinite benedictions.

Often, this is how God comes—not in rods that turn to snakes, earthquakes, or skywriting. Rather, He comes in Life which rushes at us simply by being there, ready to make connection, ready to open us up, fill us up, help us to find and believe in ourselves.

We need to touch each other often. Physical contact usually creates inward touching, too. Such tactile truth says: You are wonderful; you are beautiful; you are God's gift to me.

Here is rhythm: our reaching out to touch, followed by inward touchings that make us more human, exciting us to magnified aliveness and more confident feelings about our own worth.

This rhythm is reproduced antiphonally in the Eucharist where we touch the Word. Bread held between our fingers and wine warming our tongues make grace physical and personal.

"That which was from the beginning, which we have heard, which we have seen with our eyes, which we have looked upon and touched with our hands..." (1 John 1:1 RSV). The loaf and chalice carry us into the heart of things in ways language cannot do. Words tend to become lost in the saturation-bombing of newspapers, television, and billboards. Like the woman with the hemorrhage, we reach out our hands to touch the Word in the midst of words.

Then, the reverse happens. By touching, we ourselves are touched. Our souls are roused from sleep. The sun comes out from behind the clouds. Depressions vanish. We know the renaissance of hopefulness. Suddenly we feel more open to one another. We are more enchanted by the world and our own place in it. God is no longer a far-off mystery. He is a Presence as real as the food sliding down our throats.

In a hospital room a man was dying. He was a young man and his dying seemed so wrong. Around the bed the family was gathered, along with the grave-faced doctor and three nurses. Everything that could possibly be done to save his life had now been done. But the life was going, nevertheless. There was a long silence. Words of any kind seemed out of place. There were only tight throats and burdened hearts.

Then, as if guided from beyond, the family's young pastor, who had been standing near the back of the room, walked to the bed-table, dipped his fingers in a water glass, and made the sign of the cross on the forehead of the sleeping lad. In a dam-bursting flood of relief, with tears running down his cheeks, the father exclaimed, "Thank God!"

Touching is a link with hope, a link with God. Love's most perfect gesture.

If we are able to reach out and touch someone who loves us, someone who is ready to share whatever is inside of us, we can overcome whatever life can dish out.

And when life touches us in depths, as mysterious as the universe itself, it means God has come to remind us once again that the Kingdom of God is at hand.

There is a legend that has often been told
Of the boy who searched for the windows of gold,
The beautiful windows he saw far away
When he looked in the valley at sunrise each day,
And he yearned to go down to the valley below
But he lived on a mountain that was covered with snow
And he knew it would be a difficult trek,
But that was a journey he wanted to make,
So he planned by day and he dreamed by night
Of how he could reach THE GREAT SHINING LIGHT...
And one golden morning when dawn broke through
And the valley sparkled with diamonds of dew
He started to climb down the mountainside
With THE WINDOWS of GOLD as his goal and his guide...
He traveled all day and, weary and worn,
With bleeding feet and clothes that were torn
He entered the peaceful valley town
Just as the GOLDEN SUN WENT DOWN...
But he seemed to have lost his "GUIDING LIGHT,"
The windows were dark that had once been bright,
And hungry and tired and lonely and cold
He cried "WON'T YOU SHOW ME THE WINDOWS OF GOLD?"

And a kind hand touched him and said, "Behold!
HIGH ON THE MOUNTAIN ARE THE WINDOWS OF
GOLD"—
For the sun going down in a great golden ball
Had burnished the windows of his cabin so small,
And THE KINGDOM of GOD with its GREAT SHINING
LIGHT,
Like the GOLDEN WINDOWS that shone so bright,
Is not a far distant place, somewhere,
It's as close to you as a silent prayer—
And your search for God will end and begin
When you look for HIM and FIND HIM WITHIN.

—HELEN STEINER RICE

4
The Sacrament of Yourself

I want to be me.
I mustn't be you.
You are wonderful.
You are successful.
You are nice, and
Have a pretty face.
But I cannot be you.
And (sorry if it hurts)
I don't want
To be you.

I want to dent
The face of life somewhere,
Somehow, with my
Own mark. Even if

> I must be bad,
> That's better than
> Not being at all, or
> Trying merely to be
> Someone else.
>
> I want to crawl out
> Of the uterus of nothingness
> Into someoneness. I
> Want to sing my
> Own song, die my
> Own death. Let life
> Know that I was here
> And I did my thing.
> —JAMES W. ANGELL

A college co-ed was walking in a picket line when a corporation executive came by. "What are you doing that for?" he said. "Don't you know you can't change the world?"

She smiled and replied, "Maybe I can't change the world, but neither do I want the world to change me."

She was lucky. She has a "me" she is in touch with.

How do we identify, develop, and defend our "me"?

The need to merge into the group is strong. We enjoy the approval of peers more than anything else we can think of.

At the McCormick Seminary in Chicago we were a student family of four, living in a two-room apartment. One served as a combination kitchen-bedroom; the other as a living room and bedroom. At night, father and mother slept in one room; the two little girls in the other. One day, the four-year-old daughter of a professor with whom our children played asked at home, "Mother, may I sleep in the kitchen tonight?"

Her mother was puzzled. "Why do you want to sleep in the kitchen?"

Said Sophie, "Because Ann and Susan Angell do."

We enjoy the security of inclusion. If everyone is wearing

blue jeans or a fringed jacket, we want to wear the same. We want to be like the other kids. Parental approval or disapproval enters in only slightly. The thing really on our minds is: What will the rest of the kids think? We never outgrow that question.

Actors value most the opinion of other actors. Athletes covet the respect of other athletes.

Peer pressures are part of the miracle of community and the incentive to excellence. But sometimes peer pressures are dehumanizing and destructive. In the San Francisco Bay area there are thousands of heroin addicts, mostly under twenty-five years old. Youngsters twelve and fourteen years of age get hooked. The answer most addicts give as to why they got involved is that they were coaxed or dared into it.

Parents should realize how great peer pressures are. Any boy who has ever played in a football game and heard his name mentioned over a public address system for having made the tackle knows. Praise is the grooviest thing there is. Rejection, the hardest to absorb.

Who am I? And who's to make that decision?

In a way, this is what the minority struggle is about. "Black is beautiful" is a cry of identity—a shout uttered against an assumption, half-buried in the sleeping consciousness of society, black and white, that blackness is less desirable than whiteness. To be born with a black skin is not something anyone would deliberately choose if he could.

American Indians are now engaged in a war within themselves, a war they know they have to win inside the rink of their own emotions before they can begin to change opinions around them. The Indian is trying to start with the realization that even the name *Indian* is one assigned to him by some strangers from another land who didn't know who he was, who ignorantly associated him with the natives of India. He is saying, through Alcatraz and other haphazard movements, "I have to redefine myself. I cannot be like the pathetic figure in the Lillian Smith story who said, dejectedly, 'People like us never do anything; we just have things done to us.'"

Shall government make the Who-am-I? decisions? Films? Fashion experts? Madison Avenue? How can we find out in a way that, when pressures begin to mount, won't permit us to cave in and say, "Gee, I don't know; I guess *you'll* have to tell me"?

There are skills it will help to learn.

First, there is the poise which grows out of the remembrance that God believes in us, even in those moments when we have trouble believing in ourselves. God accepts us as we are, where we are. I am an original by Him. No one in all this world can be me, except me. No one can duplicate my contribution.

Children begin early to formulate feelings about themselves. Parents can help to shape those feelings in a positive direction by generous praise, by reminding their children of their right to be different and their right to fail. They need to affirm their children as persons for their own sakes. If parents feel good about themselves, they can relate to others from positions of strength rather than weakness. If they have definite ideas about who they are, they are also in favorable positions to help their children find out who *they* are. Families exist to confirm acceptance. Other members of our own families can make us feel there is something valuable about our life, something different, something good. Children learn how to love by being loved.

Youth do not want to be imitations of their parents, and parents should not have their egos damaged as a result of finding out their own example is not being followed.

Malvina Reynolds parodied conformity in an unforgettable way in the popular song, "Little Boxes":

> Little boxes on the hillside,
> Little boxes all the same
> There's a green one, and a pink one,
> And a blue one, and a yellow one,
> . . . .
> And they all look just the same.

And the people in the houses
All go to the university,
And they all get put in boxes
And they come out all the same.
. . . .

And they all play on the golf course
And drink their martinis dry,
And they all have pretty children
And the children go to school,
And the children go to summer camp
And then to the university,
And they all get put in boxes
And they come out all the same.

I can't feel good about myself if I am trying to be someone else. I have to be me. And I may only be able to find that "me" through the anger of rebellion.

Another useful skill is to learn how to survive without approval—to learn that there are times when that is what we must do no matter how much it hurts.

Parents need to teach their children that life is tough. It can rack us up so hard we don't know what to do. It can temper us like steel. It can send us off on an assignment into darkness. It can force us to the edge of the precipice of despair. It can dump us in with lions.

This is why the church must teach the cross. The cross of Christ is not a "pretty" to be dangled from a golden chain or bolted to a rooftop or sung about in hymns. The Christ cross is portable and painful.

There are times when we must hang tough, endure without the cheers of anyone. There are times when we must experience embarrassment, rejection, loneliness. Faith is being willing to hold on five minutes more. Peer pressure will be less threatening to those who know the story of Daniel and Good Friday, who do not come to life with the wrong expectations.

Peter says our faith is more valuable than gold, but like gold, which is imperishable, it must be purified by fire.

Still another skill is to locate references outside ourselves —references we can bank on.

The crowd doesn't pass that test. It's here today. Tomorrow it wears a different face.

Nor can we blithely say: *I'll* decide who I am. That sounds brave, but in practice isn't worth much. The Reformers would not allow a man to call himself to the ministry. He was not permitted to be the judge of himself or the presence of the Spirit.

If a man says, "I am no good," we refuse to let that self-inflicted judgment stand. If another man says, "I'm brilliant," we're apt to reject that opinion, too. Where, then, can we turn to get a correct identity bearing?

Christians use Jesus as a North Star, and the community of His love as a chart against which to check their position. The church is a fellowship in which men are continuously involved in answering for each other the question, "Who am I?" It is where people care a great deal about each other, where they are trying to convert information into truth, truth into wisdom. It is where none asks or prays or decides upon his answer alone.

The church is where different generations meet and exchange gifts of the Spirit. If we are fifteen years old, we cannot let other fifteen-year-olds answer the question, except in part. If we are seventy-five, we cannot rely solely upon the opinion of a society that lumps us thoughtlessly and inaccurately into the category of old people. What welds us all together is the one Lord and one faith, one baptism, one God and Father of us all.

Paul said: "Do not be conformed to this world" (Romans 12:2 RSV). What he meant is: Don't let anybody cram you into a little box whether it is labeled "pot smoker," "old person," or "member of the Happy Meadows Country Club." Instead, he wrote "Be transformed by the renewal of your mind."

Your life is made of stardust.

You are a stranger upon the streets of Earth.

Your true citizenship is in heaven.

Who decides who you are? The decision is already made. God made it, and it is beyond revocation. We must embrace His decision, turn it into a song which others, coming along after us, will hear being sung up ahead. From far back they will pick up the melody and start to sing it, too, and its music will never end.

II
TOMORROW JUST GOT HERE

11
TOMORROW JUST GOT HERE

5
How We Misspelled SUCCES by Really Trying

> We found no consistent relation between self-esteem and physical attractiveness, height, the size of the boy's family, early trauma, breast– or bottle–feeding in infancy or the mother's principal occupation (that is, whether she spent her time at home as a housewife or went out to work). Even more surprising, our subjects' self-esteem depended only weakly, if at all, on family social position or income level. Studies by other investigators confirm that what we observed in our boys is also true of adults: the proportion of individuals with high self-esteem is almost as high in low social classes as it is in the higher classes. Our subjects tended to gauge their individual worth primarily by their achievements and treatment in their own interpersonal environment. . . .
> —STANLEY COOPERSMITH

John Calvin called the Bible "a pair of spectacles" which men use to bring into focus the significance of what is going on in their lives. We no longer use the word *spectacles,* but we get his point. Now the metaphor would be X rays or the telephoto lens.

It is difficult to estimate success or significance or much of anything else in our own fruit-basket-upset age. Ours is a time filled both with stunning miracles and outrageous violence.

A sign in Haight-Ashbury, in the heyday of hippie-ism, read, "Due to a lack of interest, tomorrow has been cancelled." Another sign, which might well be posted on the front door of the world, reads, "If you aren't confused, you just don't understand the situation."

While our years seem to have no parallel, the Christian faith is not as unhinged by them as we are.

Lord, You have been our dwelling in *every* generation.

There are unsettled, uncertain times behind us. Though the sixties were marked by extremism and crisis, at the heart of the ferment there was, and is in the seventies, clearly something promising, something hopeful.

Not all the signs are good, and it is always easier to destroy than to create. But to write off our contemporary commotion as the silly, selfish iconoclasm of the young is to miss a stunning opportunity.

One thing we are struggling with is the effort to redefine success.

The word *success* does not appear in the New Testament, and only once or twice—in an incidental way—in the Old Testament. Still, it is a large word in modern thought, and it has much to do with feelings we have about ourselves.

Success on the playing field is winning. Politics, ditto.

A successful song is a song people want to sing over and over. Latest releases of the Rolling Stones spread across the country with the speed of light.

We know what it is to be successful in business: profit, the closed deal, expansion, conglomeration.

A successful church is one in which people are participating with enthusiasm, giving money, worshiping, working, sacrificing for something that has commanded their loyalty and love.

Success is Apollo 15. A college degree. A good home. A good education. Good clothes. A happy marriage. The respect of others. It all seems so smoglessly clear—like beyond debate.

In America success has been the order of the day for almost two hundred years. We have no interest in being second. When the word was passed from the Pentagon that our military objective is now "sufficiency," rather than "superiority," the corners of mouths curved down. We are accustomed to being superior.

In the movie *The Graduate*, Ben Braddock returns home from college. It is assumed by his family that he is interested in success. Who isn't? That B.A. degree is just the first rung on the ladder. Ben's father cannot—absolutely cannot—understand any alternatives to his own system of value. "There is, for God's sake, only one system, isn't there—only one way, one ambition common to men?"

Because most younger people understood Benjamin's feelings, and participated in them to some extent, they made *The Graduate* what *Gone With the Wind* was to the generation that preceded them.

Did you ever give a gift with the feeling it was bound to be a hit? A great choice, you thought. But it wasn't; so you wound up with an awful feeling inside of you. You couldn't blame that person. You just missed the target. You thought you knew what was wanted, what was liked. But you were mistaken. It was the wrong brand, the wrong size, the wrong color, the wrong scent.

This seems to be "where it's at" today.

Because of national affluence and technical genius, we assume it is possible for us all to be successes. We can now have all the things men have always wanted to have: money, leisure, homes in exurbia, food, stylish clothes, protection from our enemies by systems that intercept ICBMs and knock them down before they reach our shores. We can all go to college, all be men of distinction, sip bourbon in front of cozy fires with black and white Dalmatians snoozing at our feet.

But voices are crying No! No! No!

What's the matter? I thought that's what you wanted. I thought that's what you always wanted! Isn't it what *everybody* wants?

No, it isn't! It *isn't!*

Peter was a fisherman. If he were describing for us his first calling, he probably would say, "And a good one it is, too!" Success at fishing means you catch lots of fish.

But in a scene Luke paints in chapter five of his gospel,

when Peter meets Jesus for the first time, Peter is all failure. It was one of those days, or nights. "Master, we have worked all night and caught nothing!" An unsuccessful fisherman. A man with nothing to show for his labor.

Jesus could have said, "Peter, that's no good. Fishing is for the birds. See what little you have to show for all your toil. Leave this trade. Come, follow me."

And mercurial Peter would have said, "Lord, You're right. This is no good; I never wanted to be a fisherman anyway."

And Jesus would have looked at those tough hands, the creased face, and the tender mouth, and thought to Himself, "Peter you're lying in your teeth! You love fishing. Your lungs are lined with salt. And you're a competitor, too! You know how to handle men. You're a fisherman all right, but you're going to be *my* fisherman. I'm not going to take you off the bottom, though. I'm going to take you off the top."

At Jesus' bidding, the lines are reloosed and the ship pointed toward the open sea. The nets are lowered. And Luke says that when they did this, they enclosed a great multitude of fish and their nets broke. They even signaled for the men in a nearby boat to come. They came and filled their nets, too, and there was not room on board both vessels to hold the astounding catch.

From this pinnacle of achievement—in the face of this smashing success—Jesus reached out and made Peter His disciple. With Peter, He claimed James and John, also, and to those first enrollees of the intimate community that would change the world He said: "Don't worry about leaving the nets. From now on we are going to catch men!"

This was the call beyond success. Better still, the call to a new style of success.

Or maybe to the rejection of success. Jesus did not promise success. He promised hardship, the prospect of being misunderstood.

That is why the young voices of today deserve sensitive hearing.

The center of the gospel is a cross, not a thousand dollar bill.

Still, Jesus never suggested: "Let's all go out now and make a mess out of our lives. Let's be irresponsible, exalt the antihero. Let everyone get drunk or high on drugs. Let's be dirty and lazy. Let's turn off, drop out. Let someone else build the hospitals, carry the fight against muscular dystrophy, purify the air men breathe, assume the defense of liberty." That would be a denial of everything He taught from a boat. But we would not need to look far to find those who would say something like this: "I knocked myself out getting all these things. Now that I have them, I am only lonely and unhappy. I was so busy being successful I fell flat on my face as a human being. I thought I knew what I wanted—a room at the top—but that wasn't it. Not only was that not it, but in my rush to get there, I sold off a lot of things that *did* matter!"

> Whenever Richard Cory went down town,
>   We people on the pavement looked at him:
> He was a gentleman from sole to crown,
>   Clean favored, and imperially slim.
>
> And he was always quietly arrayed,
>   And he was always human when he talked;
> But still he fluttered pulses when he said,
>   "Good morning," and he glittered when he walked.
>
> And he was rich—yes, richer than a king—
>   And admirably schooled in every grace:
> In fine, we thought that he was everything
>   To make us wish that we were in his place.
>
> So on we worked, and waited for the light,
>   And went without meat, and cursed the bread;
> And Richard Cory, one calm summer night,
>   Went home and put a bullet through his head.
>   EDWIN ARLINGTON ROBINSON

Young people are trying to help redefine success. They are reexamining the premises of American existence upon oil-smeared beaches; they're aware of the depersonalized existence in cities and the expenditure of almost half of a national budget on the hostile hardware of war.

I am not willing to knock better living through chemistry, better schools, better health, better incomes. I want my marriage to be a success. I want to be a reasonable success as a father, as a minister of God, as a citizen, and as a man. I am not ashamed of such goals. But I know this: I may have the success of things, the success of appearances, power, fame, security—all of these—and still not know how to pray, how to love, how to forgive, how to feel, how to communicate, so that all there is between other men and me are the sounds of silence, the sound of money changing hands, of words passing through the air; beauty unnoticed, life at its middle, unlived.

On college and university campuses, militants comprise less than two percent of the total number of students. Students for a Democratic Society comprise less than one-tenth of one percent. What some groups aim for is the destruction of society. That goal must be denied. But we err if we equate the challenge that is being made to an old value system with anarchism. Ours is a greater malaise than that.

Older generations are being put on notice that to be successful (the word itself would be thrown out now as misleading), to be a person, a fulfilled person, is to be, first, not necessarily a winner in the eyes of the world nor locked in by someone else's definition or category. It is to be free, free to come to terms with the universe, and with yourself, and with God on your own responsibility.

It is also to be in touch with other men, to enter into, not just walk across the surface of, their lives. It is to live in such a way that other men can be in touch with you.

And it is to have discovered and tapped your capacity to love, to care, to feel, and to pour out your humanity on the altar of needs other than your own.

Youth are saying that unless this happens to us, we will

have missed the boat. This was the name of the storm blowing through the brain of Ben Braddock.

Back to the old drawing board. Or do we mean forward to the new spelling book?

6
Persons Versus Purple Cows: I'd Rather Be Than See One

> I never saw a Purple Cow,
> I never hope to see one;
> But I can tell you, anyhow,
> I'd rather see than be one.
> —GELETT BURGESS

While out of one side of our mouths we admit that material things are not a true measure of human success, we still find it hard not to be impressed by the fact that Howard Hughes is a billionaire. "Money isn't everything," said a friend piously. Then he added, "But it's way ahead of whatever's in second place!"

In our society it is still important to possess, still a sin to be poor.

As we have seen, youth have challenged the American facade of affluence and asked the question, Isn't it more important to *be* than to *have*? Isn't it the goal of existence to be human, to be just, to be sensitive to others and capable of love?

To understand this difference is to understand some of the hoopla over hair.

An elementary English lesson involves the forms of the verb *to be*: *I am; you are; he is.*

Good teachers seem to have a preference for the second person:

> *You are* light for all the world. A town that stands on a hill cannot be hidden. [Matthew 5:14 NEB]
>
> *You are* salt to the world. And if salt becomes tasteless, how is its saltness to be restored? [Matthew 5:13 NEB]
>
> *You are* my friends, if you do what I command you. [John 15:14 NEB]
>
> We are God's fellow-workers; and *you are* God's garden. [1 Corinthians 3:9 NEB]
>
> And the temple of the living God is what *we are.* [2 Corinthians 6:16 NEB]
>
> We were called God's children, and such *we are.* . . . [1 John 3:1 NEB]

(Italics in the preceding are by the author.)

The search for the meaning "beyond success" is preoccupied with two questions: Who is Man? and Who is God? Christianity doesn't believe they can be answered separately. A man who thinks of himself as a son of God will perform differently from a man who thinks of himself as a robot. Blaise Pascal said it is dangerous to show man his animal nature unless you show him his god-nature at the same time. This is just as true in reverse.

There's nothing wrong with having. We need money to buy food, to pay the druggist. It isn't wrong to want to be able to do things for and with our children, to have enough income so that we do not need to spend all our waking hours trying to figure out how to meet our bills; nor is it wrong to buy a record album or enjoy an evening out without feeling uneasy. The problem arises when we start to imagine that this is what life is principally about.

Dignity or self-respect can't be bought with money.

We can be both economically poor and greatly human.

Having and being are not dependent upon each other.

In May, 1941, I walked in a Simpson College baccalaureate procession beside former student Dr. George Washington Carver. Where this black, brilliant scientist would fit on the racial scene today is a question, but he would be a genius in any age. His voice was squeaky, then, and he more tottered than walked. He belonged to the real aristocracy of Man, and we who were students knew it.

He had come back to this small Methodist school because this was where he was eventually admitted after having been refused at another institution.

When he was a successful botanist, Carver regularly arose at four to study the secrets of nature. He would forget to cash salary checks because of his preoccupation with his experiments. When he was summoned to Washington, D.C., to testify on the agricultural problems of the South, the congressional investigative committee that had first allotted him fifteen minutes wound up listening with rapt attention for more than two hours.

Mohandas Gandhi left an estate valued at forty-six dollars. Also, an imperishable lesson about peace.

Martin Luther King, Jr., left an estate somewhat larger, but it will take a dozen generations to get their arms around his legacy.

After college and World War II, I returned to my hometown to settle down and practice law. The decision was a source of comfort and enjoyment to my parents because I was their only child. When an invitation came, not long afterward, to take a position in another state, I was concerned about their feelings. I felt sure it would mean deep disappointment. When I broke the news to my mother, she put me at ease by saying, "Take it! It's not *where* you are that matters; only *what* you are."

Deciding upon which image we are willing to settle for,

live with, the question "Who am I?" translates into "*whose am I?*"

It is part of Christian identity to accept this fact: "You are not your own; you were bought with a price" (1 Corinthians 6:19,20 RSV).

To be a Christ-owned person is to place high on your agenda the matter of learning how to be fully and enthusiastically human.

It isn't as easy as it sounds, but if John Killinger could do it, you can, too. In *For God's Sake, Be Human,* he retraces for us his own journey along Liberation Road:

> I confess that I too have joined the concert of voices against overmuch individualism in religion and have insisted at times on almost a coherence among believers, a submergence of self in the corporate church, in the body of saints in all the ages. But I remember now with much pointedness that my own attachment to the church, that has since circumscribed my life, began in those bittersweet hours of late adolesence when I stopped by a gurgling brook or watched the moon in a fishpond or sat on a high hill looking at the world with God and thinking what I must do for him to make it all his again. I didn't live a day then without walking and talking with him (are the hymn lyrics so far-fetched?) without laughing and crying in the wind, without feeling like a young animal caught up in the rhythms of nature.
>
> That was all very juvenile, of course, and I have since learned to curb the I, to muffle it and gag and drug it and deter it and denature it until it is quite unsure of itself, sickened and humiliated and nearly destroyed. But not quite. It survives. And sometimes it revives. Sometimes it waxes again, and for a moment I feel something surging back, something like health or strength or power or excitement, some-

thing like life; and I wonder if I have not been wrong to hedge it and hurt it, to squelch and welch on it, to bang it and bury it—if, maybe, it is not the better part of me, the only real part of me, the only real thing I have to give to the world or to God, the single, sole essence of what lives in my house and calls itself by my name. I wonder, in short, if I have not been guilty of murder, if I have not taken by suicide the life that God gave me to live and enjoy in the world.

Christian identity also involves being the gracious neighbor.

Tom Martin spoke to his congregation one Sunday morning on "Your Nearest Neighbor." According to Tom, he is our wife, our husband, our child, our father, our mother. We do not usually think of those who are bound up so closely with us in the bundle of life as neighbors.

Belief means to "be-in-life."

God is not an ethereal ectoplasm stationed somewhere between Saturn and Mars. He meets us, ministers to us, speaks to us, comforts us *through* persons as limited and as fallible as ourselves. For early men of faith, God had His dwelling upon a high mountain. Around the peak lightning would flash and smoke would swirl. Then God left the mountain and took up residence in the Temple. This didn't last either. God cannot be domesticated. He can only be revealed in the mysteries of stars and persons.

One night, when the sky was jet velvet, Jesus and Nicodemus sat on a rooftop talking. Part of this sublime and long-remembered conversation was Jesus' remark about the divine methodology: "The wind blows where it wills; you hear the sound of it, but you do not know where it comes from, or where it is going. So with everyone who is born from spirit" (John 3:8 NEB).

There is no waiting list for being human, for being the gracious neighbor or the instrument of glorious Kindness.

A silly poem about purple cows says, "I'd rather see than be one." Christian discipleship won't let us off with looking. It is the imperative *be*.

At the close of a theatre performance, an amnesia sufferer hurried onto the stage as the houselights came up. Looking out over the sea of startled faces, he asked with earnest emotion, "Can anyone tell me who I am?"

I can. You are the unique creation of a still creating God. You are part of a royal family. You are a piece of the new humanity.

7
Has God Changed His Mind About Sex?

As we live, we are transmitters of life,
And when we fail to transmit life, life fails to flow
   through us.
That is part of the mystery of sex, it is a flow
   onwards.
And if, as we work, we can transmit life into our
   work, life, still more life, rushes into us to
   compensate, to be ready, and we ripple with life
   through the days.
Even if it is a woman making an apple dumpling, or a
   man a stool, if life goes into the pudding, good
   is the pudding, good is the stool . . .
Give, and it shall be given unto you is still the
   truth about life. But giving life is not so easy.
   It doesn't mean handing it out to some mean fool,
   or letting the living dead eat you up.

> It means kindling the life-quality, where it was not, even if it's only in the whiteness of a washed pocket handkerchief.
>
> —D. H. LAWRENCE

A generation ago Peter Marshall, then pastor of The New York Avenue Presbyterian Church in Washington, D.C., preached a sermon to his congregation called "The Powder Keg." The powder keg was, and is, that ever-popular commodity, sex.

Sex is a loaded cannon that is likely to go off without warning and leave us with a hand or a leg missing.

Explicit movies; books like *Portnoy's Complaint* and David Reuben's *Everything You Always Wanted to Know About Sex and Were Afraid to Ask;* homosexual parades; liberalized abortion laws; letters from college reading, "Dear Mom, I know you won't understand this, but Paul and I have started living together"; and the whole biochemical revolution in birth regulation have produced a moral storm. People disagree about Viet Nam, hair, skirt lengths, or whether we should spend more money on space, but that is mild compared to the volatile attitudes people hold about sexuality.

It is an explosive topic about an explosive force in man.

Sex, though, has to do with more than what happens to people in bedrooms. It is part of a deeper mystery: the mystery of personhood. Sexual difficulties, where they exist, usually show us only the tip of an iceberg. They are facade. Back of talk about incompatibility usually are hurts, hungers, confusions about self-worth, deferred but significant ambitions, questions about love and hate and freedom, and the yearning to be taken seriously as a human being.

Today, the mores of the presixties are undergoing harsh review. The changes, though, began long before that. Probably few of us remember a time when it was considered immodest for a woman to walk about with exposed ankles, but there ought to be many readers who will recall when mixed swimming between boys and girls was regarded as improper. The automobile changed things. Radio, television, wars, science, bikinis, the shattering of old authority structures—a whole new world has been cascading down since the end of World War I. The falls of change are still running noisily and full of foam.

The Bible mentions sex in some of its first paragraphs and says that it is good.

In the Greek view, man's soul was his "good" part. Flesh was evil. Physical feelings tended to corrupt the career of the soul. Christianity takes an opposite view. It overturned the older position by declaring that God *became* flesh and came to men. It does not tiptoe around sex, nor is it reluctant to admit people are made the way they are. There is no conspiracy of silence in a truly contemporary version of Christian faith. It sees sex as a gift.

The first instruction God gave to Adam and Eve was: "Be fruitful and multiply, and fill the earth and subdue it" (Genesis 1:28 RSV). Clearly, God has given man a part of the creative action.

Why have we allowed our sexuality to become the basis for so many feelings about guilt and shame? Why have we demanded that our children live in a split-level world where most of life is normal and good, but sex a naughty secret?

Perhaps some of the worry associated with sex education is centered in the awareness that mechanical information in itself is not enough of a basis on which to respond to the inward fire. There is a lack of confidence that the surrounding contexts of meaning and decision are furnished along with the hard facts.

Sam Levenson has a little girl saying to a little boy, "Let's play pregnant. You shave and I'll throw up."

Carefulness in dealing with sex can amount to prudery, the handing on of baseless fears. But not necessarily so. If you had a hundred dollar bill you would be careful what you did with it. You wouldn't leave it in a junk drawer or the glove compartment. Sexual nature is like that, too. Anyone who understands sexual encounter as no more significant than eating a dish of ice cream is more dumb than immoral. Such an attitude reveals not an obsessiveness but a deadness to life. It is in an affliction which quickly spreads to everything: to the elegance of nature, the wonder of children, the magnificence of music, the struggle for justice.

The Bible has a marvelous way of describing sexual intercourse. It speaks of it as "knowing" another person. Sex involves the power to create and the power to love. That's what sex is about. When one, or both, elements are missing, all that's left of the circus is the sawdust and the deserted bleachers.

The Christian faith declares that men and women were created to take responsibility for each other, and the story of Adam's rib is a diamond-studded footnote. In the sparkle of that myth we behold something both romantic and profound about men and women. It has been said concerning the story: "Woman was taken out of man; not out of his head to top him, nor out of his feet to be trampled underfoot; but out of his side to be equal to him, under his arm to be protected, and near his heart to be loved."

There is also a mixture of beauty and horse sense in these words: ". . . the head of every man is Christ; and the head of the woman is the man; and the head of Christ is God. . . . as the woman is of the man, even so is the man also by the woman; but all things of God" (1 Corinthians 11:3,12 KJV).

We express responsibility for each other, or decline it, by way of sex. Man and woman are the first building blocks of community. The Bible moves from the story of the first man and first woman to the story of Cain and Abel. The thread which unites these two narratives is the thread of responsibility one person has for another.

Today's rhubarb over sex represents the concern of a new strain of young men and women who are not as iconoclastic as they are in earnest about qualities of human relationship and who, often in imitation of Jesus, are saying that asking whether or not something is legal is not asking the most important question.

The new moralists say that they resent a *single-question approach* as a realistic measurement of rightness or wrongness in intersexual conduct. Whether the subject is chastity of single people or adultery by married people, the one-question approach is: "Did you or didn't you?" Have you crossed this all-the-way magic line that separates purity from guilt, continence from transgression?

Raising the question is not meant to imply that chastity is obsolete or that Hugh Hefner is a prophet. It is rather that, in evaluating relationships between people, in assessing the morality or immorality of behavior, we assign a terrible amount of weight to one point, and that fixation blinds us to other things. Sex is not the only moral issue on the line in modern society, though we sometimes act as if it were. Among banned California prefixes for automobile license plates, SEX is out, but WAR is in.

In marriage, two people may commit psychological mayhem. They may see the complete disappearance between them of what the marriage service calls "mutual esteem and love." Their marriage may spiritually die, be filled with what one novelist has called innumerable "plastic ironies." They may lie, hate, cut, abuse, annihilate each other as human beings. But as long as it goes on behind the barrier of a ceremony someone uttered in front of them one lazy afternoon in May, society has a way of folding its hands and calling the game "fair."

Rather than arguing that sexual experience is such a "big deal," and so pleasurable they demand access to it with no limitations involved, younger critics accuse the older view of being fanatical about sex, and with letting sexual intercourse obscure all kinds of other values which also need to act as a gauge of whether or not people are authentically alive.

A second protest says that a *strictly legal approach* to ethics is no more commendable when it comes to sex than it is to the man who cheats his neighbor, then waves the small print of the contract in his face and says, "Ah, you see, you signed that. You're stuck, my friend. Read what it says right there at the bottom!"

It would be silly to suggest that contracts are not necessary, or that order and discipline are not important in human experience. But Christians do not stop their reading with the Old Testament. Jesus calls His followers to life so engulfed by feelings of love and gratitude that requirements of the law are left behind. His question is: "What do you do *more* than others?"

Paul speaks of the law as the "schoolmaster" who leads men to Christ, but he emphasizes that the law cannot, of itself, shape us into the children of God.

In the case of a person charged with homosexuality, in the prevailing view in our society, there is one, lonely criterion: guilty or not guilty? If the party is adjudged guilty, he becomes a marked person, a social misfit, someone vulnerable to blackmail, and, on that account, undeserving of public trust. Is this the price a person ought to pay for violating the social compact—that our chief concern needs to be the protection of the heterosexual community from further infection? What is infinitely valuable in the universe are not principles but persons. The teachings of Jesus are a better basis for assessing sin than customs.

Another criticism leveled at the existing system says *it is unreasonable to treat everyone who doesn't fit a certain pattern as odd.*

The Christian ideal is, admittedly, the happy family—father, mother, children—living together in harmony and permanency of relationship. But millions and millions of people are not in such a situation. They could not be if they wanted to. In the United States there are twenty million women without men. There are single men. Some are young, some middle-aged, some older. There are widows, and widowers. These people have their sexuality to account for, too.

The new perspective on sex is not interested in tearing down the ideal marriage and ideal family. It is trying to use a wider lens than the one the past has used to say something intelligent and honest about sex beyond the model of the completed family.

A fourth issue involves *permanency*. Marriage in Christ has generally been understood to be permanent: "To love and to cherish till death do us part" or "in joy and in sorrow, in sickness and in health, as long as we both shall live." One man and one woman in lifelong unity and love. That is where the church has stood, still stands, in expressing the will of God.

It would be easy to quit there and say that anything less than permanence is failure. The ideal has served us well, and I could not suggest that two people, contracting a marriage, strive for less. But this could lead into still another legalistic trap. Marriages which last are marriages to be respected. But merely to survive the obstacle course is hardly worth being counted among life's top virtues.

At a golden wedding reception, a bride of fifty years was asked if she had ever thought of divorce. "No," she replied. "Murder? Yes." In addition to durability, we must go on and ask: What happened to the persons involved during the marriage? Is it still fulfilling its purpose? A family I know is dissolving a union after thirty-four years. Everyone is wringing his hands and feeling badly. It is an occasion of broad regret. Yet, most of us know little or nothing about what those thirty-four years add up to, or failed to add up to.

We are being challenged to ask more than the one question: Did it last? Permanence in marriage is good, but only if other good things are present and continue to be celebrated between persons.

There is enough truth in what is being said to cause everyone to do some hard thinking. What we need, as in the case of most of our divisions, is not victory on one side but synthesis.

Having attempted to understand one side of the morality debate, let's take a look at the opposite side.

If there is substance to the argument that the one-question approach to sexual manners has an element of phoniness in it, that question does suggest that responsible people cannot treat intercourse *only* recreationally. If life is sacred, the life-forming process is also sacred.

Prostitution is a disaster, a gross failure of what it is we were put on earth to become. People who engage in sex apart from the commitment of themselves walk around the rim of hell. The so-called magic line which the new morality is questioning may represent a crucial line of defense for the human spirit.

Morality cannot exist without lines. A man who works in a bank must draw a line between his own money and the money that doesn't belong to him, and that line must be black and clear.

Most of us still need rules to live by and the stabilities of marriage to keep us from making awful fools of ourselves. Rule morality can hide hypocrisy, but it may also save the ship. To say our prayers regularly doesn't mean we always pray well, or even sincerely, but by making prayer a rule of our lives there's at least a good chance that occasionally we will.

Morality, though, is written in men's hearts rather than in the stars.

We can expect changes in permanency of relationship. One minister has changed the marriage vow from "till death do us part" to "so long as we are able."

Permanency of relationship costs a lot in courage, but it is worth the price. Once, one of our daughters came home from high school and commented on a couple of sophomores who had eloped the month before. "They're so happy!" she said, half enviously. Three months later both youngsters were living back at home. Lasting marriage contains rich rewards, especially for children who grow up securely and with firm examples to copy.

Has God changed His mind about sex? There's no way to answer that question, but changes are in the wind. Some promise to be good ones. The Christian faith is not only big enough to absorb them; indirectly it has produced them.

A man planted a bed of pansies. Every day he enjoyed looking at their purple and yellow faces, sometimes picking a bouquet for his desk. One day a stranger came along and told him they were not flowers but a form of oriental weed. He tore up the garden and raked the dirt smooth. That only made him feel worse. In time he paved the square of earth over with asphalt, contenting himself with telling friends that the pansies had been a delusion and that, based upon the scientific data of his friend, he had decided to eliminate their influence from his life.

God made sex as a good, and all our manuals on how it's done ought not to be allowed to wipe away its wonder. It is interwoven with the mystery of selfhood. It is part of the total interaction of persons—conversation, shared experiences, delight in the presence of one another. A man discovers what manliness is in the presence of a woman; a woman makes a similar discovery in the presence of a man. No less than our very humanity is at stake.

There was a time when society itself surrounded us with lots of stop-and-go lights. More and more we must now rely upon our own inward guidance systems as we make our way through a clutter of *Playboy,* "Topless for Lunch," and *Myra Breckenridge* toward sexual sanity. Some of the old guidelines were silly. Others plain wrong. But many were, and are, right. They have their roots in the centuries and in the Word of Life. But the world is increasingly standardless, and we must take responsibility for our choices. This makes the doctrine of the Holy Spirit the church's most important teaching.

This, rather than depressing us, ought to inspire us with the thought that the same freedom Jesus used in deciding to go to Jerusalem is still around. With that freedom, comes the chance to wring our own version of greatness out of these bewildering and beautiful years.

8
America Is Still Being Born

If we imagine the whole of earth's history compressed into a single year, then on this scale, the first eight months of the year would be completely without life. The following two months would see only the most primitive of creatures, ranging from viruses and single-celled bacteria to jellyfish, while mammals would not have appeared until the second week in December. Man as we know him would have come onto the stage at about 11:45 P.M. on December 31. The age of written history would have occupied little more than the last 60 seconds on the clock.

—RICHARD CARRINGTON

America, like our own selfhood, is not a set quality.

We can't "carry moonbeams home in a jar," and we can't take one version of the American dream, whether it's Betsy Ross, Pearl Harbor, Thomas Jefferson, or Dwight Eisenhower, and freeze it for all time.

America is more an idea than a country. America is still being born.

The Christian faith, too, is not a matter of arriving at a fixed position, but a process. To be a Christian is to be involved in becoming more than we are.

Dr. John Orr, chairman of the University of Southern California Department of Religion and Ethics, contends that most modern people today do not think of themselves as representing eternal souls, fixed and static. They see themselves, rather, as selves-in-emergence.

We live in a time when most of our images of God are unsatisfactory. We are trapped between the conclusion that God is dead and the only slightly better argument that the only God left is a God of the gaps, a God who presides over a few still unplundered territories.

In spite of limited language and inadequate images, though, many of us still believe that God *is* and that He is not a tired old man but a vigorous young Presence who is still deeply involved in the chemistry of our becoming.

No one has dared to represent God in the theatre of the imagination as someone young and muscular. If we indulge in anthropomorphism at all, it is to make God old, bent, and full of problems. This is misleading. God must be understood as the Lord of Now, not the Patron of Yesterday.

Life is eternally new. Even the life of our families, which may seem reasonably set, is packed with constant, invisible movement and change.

Paul Tillich says that we come from the darkness of the "not yet" and rush toward the darkness of the "no more." The present evaporates in the moment we are naming it "the present."

We are moving. The earth is spinning at a speed of about 1000 miles an hour. Blood rushes through our bodies. Cells swirl within our blood. Our lives are lashed rafts bouncing along upon the white turbulence of history. And our becomingness is sometimes frightening. No wonder someone exclaimed, "Stop the world! I want to get off!"

Barry Wood of Stanford University wrote in *The Magnificent Frolic:*

> The universe is not a creation, in the sense of something completed and final, but rather a continual process of creating and evolving. The isolation of things as if they were static and permanent is a useful procedure for analysis but is ultimately untrue to the facts. What we call things turn out to be, in the long view, processes—though we cannot, perhaps, be blamed for the mistake. We gaze at the sky, at constellations unchanged since first charted by Babylonian astronomers, and unwittingly think that the stars last forever. Yet even the stars grow and develop and die leaving an enrichment behind.

Speed up the camera a million times and the mountains rise, fall and erode like drifting snow; speed it up a few million more times and the stars swell and burst like children's balloons. Everything turns out to be a dynamic process of change—a kind of magic we say.

The same is true of human bodies and minds. We grow out of the sea and soil, and our blood streams flow with the saltiness of primeval oceans from which we came. "All is change," said the Greek philosopher Heraclitus. "Only change is changeless." Man is not explainable as a being, for he is an eddy of star dust, a constant becoming.

Flux is the only way we can understand either our country or ourselves. That's fine! That's what it is we are most anxious to protect: not the results or achievements of any one generation or era, but the ferment we call *freedom*. The free heart, the free mind, the free association, the free word, free movement. Freedom to engage in peaceful dissent. Freedom to strike. Freedom to change what is, by whatever steps, do not violate the process. Freedom to affirm, to deny, to be left alone. Freedom which allows another person to be himself in exchange for the right to be ourselves.

In the beginning God *began* to create the world. But He isn't through.

In 1776 America was a radical idea. In the 1860s America was a regional crisis. In the 1920s America was Charles A. Lindbergh, the Charleston, Samuel Gompers, a gadget called a radio. Some of the past remains; some has disappeared. In the sixties, more metamorphosis, more movement. In these first minutes of the seventies, already the sixties are beginning to seem like dying remembrances.

We can't go home again.

Our call is to write the new history of America, at the same time that we keep prominently posted on the kiosks of our minds such words as these:

We hold these Truths to be self-evident, that all Men are created equal, that they are endowed by their Creator with certain unalienable Rights, that among these are Life, Liberty, and the Pursuit of Happiness —That to secure these Rights, Governments are instituted among Men, deriving their just Powers from the Consent of the Governed, that whenever any Form of Government becomes destructive of these Ends, it is the Right of the People to alter or to abolish it . . . [The Declaration of Independence]

Observe good faith and justice toward all nations. Cultivate peace and harmony with all. Religion and morality enjoin this conduct. And can it be that good policy does not equally enjoin it? It will be worthy of a free, enlightened, and at no distant period a great nation to give to mankind the magnanimous and too novel example of a people always guided by an exalted justice and benevolence. [Washington's Farewell Address]

Tyranny, like hell, is not easily conquered; yet we have this consolation within us, that the harder the conflict, the more glorious the triumph. What we obtain too cheap, we esteem too lightly. . . . [Thomas Paine]

With malice toward none; with charity for all; with firmness in the right, as God gives us to see the right, let us strive to finish the work we are in; to bind up the nation's wounds; to care for him who shall have borne the battle, and for his widow and his orphan —to do all which may achieve and cherish a just and lasting peace among ourselves and with all nations. [Lincoln's Second Inaugural Address]

New forms of national maturity and greatness are being called for. The Stars and Stripes must mean new things in the 1970s.

We can honor the past without letting it become a cave in which to hide from the urgencies of a new time. Polarization sounds ugly, but free people must live with division; they must learn the creative usefulness of those tensions out of which the mutations of justice and truth come.

If America reaches the point where we no longer have freedom to speak out in opposition to the government, it will no longer make any difference who wins the Asian war.

In the second half of the sixties we held some discussions about national goals. They were inconclusive and probably would be again.

Except for a few short-term objectives, we cannot even imagine where it is we are trying to get to. The goal recedes as we approach it. The lesson from these abortive efforts is that it is not goals that matter. Only the commitment to become—to homestead the future on the open and painful edges of truth.

America can continue to grow if she will protect three assumptions.

First, life is holy. We are responsible creatures and have a Reference beyond ourselves for what we do with the world, with our time, and our opportunities.

And this: Men are brothers.

Finally, we are not alone. God is with Man.

Some say that the golden age of America is already over. Things looked great for awhile, but now America's sun is falling into the sea. She will soon be only another civilization that drowns by refusing to give up her perversions.

I cannot agree. Too many people care, and the yeast is still working.

I was startled, in visiting Rome, to be reminded that Rome was already eight hundred years old when Jesus was born. A few cities are even older. This makes New York, Chicago, Los Angeles, and Philadelphia dirty-faced kids in short pants.

I'll make it even stronger. I'll put it this way. America is still at the hospital waiting to be brought home.

III
I WONDER AS I WANDER

9
And to Think We Found You in the Yellow Pages!

When he returned one evening, he asked me anxiously: "Is there a God—yes or no? What d'you think, boss? And if there is one—anything's possible—what d'you think he looks like?"
    I shrugged my shoulders.
    "I'm not joking boss. I think of God as being exactly like me. Only bigger, stronger, crazier. And immortal, into the bargain. He's sitting on a pile of soft sheepskins and his hut's the sky. It isn't made out of old petrol-cans like ours is, but clouds. In his right hand he's holding not a knife or a pair of scales—those [awful] instruments are meant for butchers and grocers—no, he's holding a large sponge full of water, like a rain cloud. On his right is Paradise, on his left Hell. Here comes a soul; the poor little thing quite naked. God looks at it, laughing up his sleeve, but he plays the bogey man: 'Come here,' he roars, 'come here, you miserable wretch!'
    "And he begins his questioning. The naked soul throws itself at God's feet. 'Mercy!' it cries. 'I have sinned.' And away it goes reciting its sins. It recites a whole rigamarole and there's no end to it. God thinks this is too much of a good thing. He yawns. 'For heaven's sake stop!' he shouts. 'I've heard enough of all that!' Flap! Slap! A wipe of the sponge, and he washes out all the sins. 'Away with you, clear out, run off to Paradise!' he says to the soul. 'Peterkin, let this poor little creature in, too!'
    "Because God, you know is a great lord, and that's what being a lord means: to forgive!"

—NIKOS KAZANTZAKIS

It was New Year's Eve when the telephone rang in the manse. At the other end of the line was a young man who asked if a marriage might be performed within the next two or three hours. He would leave for Viet Nam within a week.

The pastor explained that he and his wife had arranged a festive evening in their home and that the guests were already beginning to arrive.

"Would it be okay if we came to your home?" asked the prospective groom. "We'd be happy if your guests would be witnesses to the service, too—if they wouldn't mind."

The wedding took place with all the guests joining in the unexpected celebration. What had begun as an almost lonely affair suddenly became a widely shared joy. As the couple raced from the manse kitchen, the bride exclaimed radiantly, "And to think we found you in the yellow pages!"

While this is not suggested as the ideal way to schedule a marriage service, its delectable element of surprise is characteristic of the life of faith.

Bethlehem was a surprise.

The cross, which looked like tragedy, had unimaginable consequences.

Paul, who guarded the piled-up coats of the sweating, angry bunch that stoned Stephen to death for his Christian faith, later wrote the words: "So faith, hope, love abide, these three; but the greatest of these is love" (1 Corinthians 13:13 RSV).

Life is a set of yellow pages, an explosion of wonder.

Childhood is a continuous wonder, when even such a thing as a dog's tongue, hanging out on a hot day, evokes awe in a two-year-old.

Rachel Carson, whose books have recaptured a sense of the miracle that lies beneath all created things, tells in *The Sense of Wonder* how she took her twenty-month-old nephew, Roger, to see the ocean for the first time.

> One stormy autumn night . . . I wrapped him in a blanket and carried him down to the beach in the rainy darkness. Out there, just at the edge of where-

we-couldn't-see, big waves were thundering in, dimly seen white shapes that boomed and shouted and threw great handfuls of froth at us. Together we laughed for pure joy—he a baby meeting for the first time the wild tumult of Oceanus, I with the salt of half a lifetime of sea love in me.

Wonder was given back to all of us in the mid-twentieth century with our extension into space.

Ray Bradbury prefaces his *Martian Chronicles* with the epigram:

> "It is good to renew one's wonder," said the philosopher. "Space travel has again made children of us all."

Even so, a space ship traveling at the fantastic speeds achieved by Apollo, would take over 200,000 years to reach the nearest star.

My astronomer friend, John Irwin, imagines a phone call between Earth and Alpha Centauri. "It could take you eight years," he said, "to find out you have dialed the wrong number!"

Socrates says philosophy begins in wonder.

Faith is a question mark as well as a declaration.

John F. Kennedy called the space the "new ocean," but with all of our midcourse corrections and those first tire tracks on the moon, there is a growing feeling in a man that it may be within the wonder of his own soul where the greatest discoveries of all remain to be made.

Author Sam Keen talks about two models of man. He uses Greek mythology to help us pinpoint important truths about ourselves. From his discussion we are able to learn something helpful about our sensitivity to wonder or deadness to its power.

Apollo, the prototype of model 1, is the god of order, reason, moderation, and balance. He is the god of prudence and discipline. From him is derived the maxim, "Know yourself."

Know yourself to be a man, limited in time and space. Do not commit the sin of pride. Do not aspire to the conditions of the gods themselves. Accept your situation.

Apollonian man has no time for foolishness. He spends his money wisely, goes to bed when people are supposed to go to bed. He works hard and worships common sense. The household of Apollo woman is tidy. In its exaggerated expression, the house may be in such apple-pie order that visitors are afraid to sit down. Nothing is out of place. Dress is always in good taste. Not too far ahead of times; not too far behind.

Americans are strongly traited by Apollo. We believe in order, stability, boundaries, individual responsibility, and peace. We have trouble understanding people who are wasteful, nonconforming or not as concerned with possession and order as we are.

The other god is Dionysus. He is model 2. He is a strange and wild deity. One of his ilk is Prometheus who sneaks across a boundary and steals fire.

Dionysian man is not courtesy or niceness; he is devilishness and thrives on ecstatic participation in the universe without uptight feelings of ego, reputation, responsibility. Rather than building structures for his grandchildren to enjoy, he is busy tearing structures down and laughing at himself.

He is opposed to having life all blocked out and sensible. He sees life as the *entrechat* rather than the marathon. He exalts freedom over authority, love over law. Behaving himself and earning gold stars for being good is not his theory of life.

He is our Uncle Louie who the family was ashamed of for getting drunk so often. The kids, by the way, loved him.

He is all of us, at times, who are tired of cages, hungry for the sky. He is Mr. X, the bus driver who one day tired of his route and headed down the road toward Key West, whistling.

If God is pleased with us when we are controlled, responsible, careful, and discreet, He also loves us when He sees in us that which is untamed and restless, so defiant of prudence that we throw away a life at age thirty-three instead of making a deal to save ourselves. Ethics has room for the prodigal as well as for the elder brother who stayed home and kept out of trouble.

This is part of the human equation—part of the mystery of being a self. Who could deny that such a quality of daring did not figure in Christianity's replacement of circumcision and rules with a new spirit of freedom and expendability?

If we have no use for discipline, life becomes chaotic, enslaving. There is wonder in order, a truth for which the universe itself is Exhibit A. Many of today's turned-on flower children are discovering that hepatitis and promiscuity are not attractive alternatives to stable marriages, good health, and shared responsibility for the politics upon which the shape of society depends.

On the other hand, thousands of human beings are living lives of "quiet desperation" because, "Dear Abby, we cannot break out of the fears, the dullness of our marriage, the boredom of our jobs, the barrenness of our hidden hearts." For some, every dream has died. To try to speak to these people of wonder would earn a bitter, cynical laugh.

We become wondering and wonder-full people by claiming the best of both worlds.

We lose the ability to wonder if, as Apollo-like men, we see all of life in pragmatic, utilitarian terms. We blunt our capacity for wonder when our main concern is that our children are copies of us and that tomorrow is supposed to be a facsimile of yesterday.

We also forfeit wonder if, as Dionysian men, we reject the tough questions and hard realities of existence and resort to playing fantasy games. This means we are not ready to take the world seriously. We forfeit wonder if, ignoring the hard choices, which are the basis of enduring love and character and leadership in faith, we enter *anomie*—that gray waste country in which there are no norms, no limits, no goals.

A movie was billed as an "un-moral picture." This is the society and life-style some would settle for. An existence in which there is no final significance, no depth, no God, no transcendent hope. Only distractions in which to try to forget the shallowness and selfishness of most of what we do.

Sam Keen said, "In spite of the skeptical star, I have never ceased to live in amazement." If we can say the same thing about ourselves, the living God cannot be far away.

10
Let's Dress Up and Play Life

Dress is the table of your contents.
—JOHN CASPAR LAVATER

A king gave a dinner in honor of his son's marriage.

When many of the guests failed to arrive, the king sent soldiers into the streets to draft whoever they could find so that all the tables would be filled. The banquet hall was soon crowded and this made the king happy. Things were going to be successful after all! The musicians were playing. The waiters were hurrying about their duties. Excitement was building.

Then the king noticed something that distressed him—a guest who had shown up in shabby clothes.

Instead of sending one of his servants over to speak to the man about the breach of etiquette, the king himself went over and scolded him.

The man was so flustered he couldn't say a word. He left the hall shaken, hurt, and confused.

This story, reported in Matthew's Gospel, doesn't end the way we would expect. If, in the parable, God is represented by the king, we would not expect petty attention to attire, nor a lack of sympathy for someone poor.

Parables ordinarily contain a single point, and it is generally thought that the point Jesus tries to make here is that God's invitation is not to be taken lightly. We do not respond to Him at our own convenience, or without being aware that God has honored us by asking us to be part of His Kingdom. We come to God with our best self, believing no other personal priority is more urgent than this one.

Whether this is what Jesus was getting at, we cannot be sure, but the story is a good starting place to discuss a theology of clothes.

One evening in the late 1950s, I drove along Mason-Headley Road in the rain on my way to a committee meeting. I flipped on the car radio hoping to catch the ball scores or find some music for relaxing.

Instead, I heard the voice of Fulton Sheen, Roman Catholic bishop, who was then as popular with radio and television audiences as Johnny Carson is now. Bishop Sheen was speaking about how style of dress expresses personality, even faith.

Ah, but here's my destination. Touch the brakes. Stop the engine, switch off car lights. I listen a few moments longer to the dramatic voice of the bishop. Click. And I am left only with an idea that would stroll up and down my mind the next ten years.

Who could have imagined then how radical and expressive, how theological, clothes would become!

Sheen said that overdress by earlier generations often concealed inward emptiness. A high-necked costume could hide all kinds of insecurity.

We probably communicate more by our dress than we know. Our garb usually registers whether we are severe, sensual, doubtful, or daring—whether we like things the way they are or would like to see them changed.

New clothes on Easter Day are meant to symbolize new life, the death of death and the return of joy.

The somber dress of the Amish—the women's bonnets and

the men's big black hats—represent a rejection of modern civilization with its materialism and speed.

The primitive style of hippies is another message about rejection—the rejection of traditional values, institutions, and centers of authority. That it has succeeded so well in throwing the Establishment off balance means that the message has gotten through.

John Holt, teacher and author of education reform books including *How Children Fail*, suggests this experiment. Let your hair grow long or get a reasonable realistic wig. Dress in authentic hippie clothes. Get a little scruffy and dirty. Then, he says, walk about in the streets of whatever city you live. What you will see in the faces of a good many people is: "If I could, I would kill you!"

Clothing communicates sorrow. Black means the darkness of the soul. White equals antiseptic. Policeman's blue, loyalty.

Children play dress-up, which means: By this miracle I am grown up.

In Exodus Moses gives instructions for the outfitting of the priests who are to preside over the worship of God in the tabernacle. Specification of colors comment upon the beauty of God and man's desire to echo that beauty with his most elegant creations.

Formal occasions—life's Camelot moments—call for still another order of raiment.

Hal March of early TV fame died early in 1970. A few weeks before his death he said with a twinkle, "I figure I was born naked and I'll go out of this world in a blue suit."

One of today's most obvious clothes messages is: I want to be free. The gray flannel suit has the badge of conformity. It seemed to say: Life is all getting ahead—getting a bigger house, a bigger salary, a bigger car. Eventually, a bigger divorce settlement. The clothes revolution which hit the scene in the 1960s said: Life is too standardized, too predictable. Life is not just that bigger income and retirement annuity. It says there is too much pretending in life. Men living in fear of what others think.

The new clothes say: Life isn't meant to be gray. It is meant to be pink, yellow, and full of psychedelic swirl. People are not meant to be all alike. Every human being is a special creation. Unique. Don't frustrate God by being afraid to do your thing because you're afraid of socially accepted images. Scrape off the veneer. Let your real self unfold; let it flower; let it be. This is good medicine for anyone to take two teaspoons of.

Clothes also mean: We want to be known.

Today's emphasis on nudity, after allowances are made for the sex merchant and the voyeur, is an attempt to get behind the masks, the veils, beneath the trappings that conceal us from each other as living persons. For some the reality has been layered over so thickly, and for so long, it has been forgotten. All there is left to do is to blush and feel threatened. Nudity though, usually misfires because one of the reasons we wear clothes in the first place is to express a mystique of personhood. We wear clothes for protection. But Genesis has this message, too. The mystery of God and man are the same mystery. Clothes help to celebrate the mystery of man. Nudity is a poor solution to the need we have to be known.

Some four-letter words are vital for understanding the three-letter word *sex*—words like care, help, kill, feel, give, and love. These constitute a Christian graffiti which, for two thousand years, has set a people apart.

A third message which is hidden in our wide ties, body shirts, miniskirts, and flare-bottom pants is that we want to be loved. Our clothes say: I want to be admired, accepted, wanted.

When we try to dress interestingly, attractively—while staying within our budgets—we are involved in the process of presenting ourselves to the world as human beings in search of acceptance. We don't want the world to club us in the face. We want to be wanted. We want to be loved but not for what we wear; what we wear is our invitation to get acquainted.

Jesus' garments add up, not the message of any one time but of all time.

Two items especially interest the storyteller of the passion narrative. One is a purple robe which the soldiers put on Jesus to mock Him in His role as King of the Jews. Apparently this was a random cloak—possibly grabbed from a passerby to go along with the mock crown, the twisted circle of thorn branches. The other garment was Jesus' usual dress —the plain tunic which John said was woven without a seam. There were four soldiers and His possessions were divided four ways. But the main garment could not be equally divided without ripping it and ruining it, so the new owner had to be determined by a throw of the dice.

The story of the man who won the throw of the dice was created by Lloyd Douglas. In his dedication to *The Robe,* Douglas credits Hazel McCann for raising the question and setting him to wonder what became of the robe.

For Christians the purple robe has become the clue to whatever authentic royalty there is within mankind.

That the clothes of Christ wound up in four piles, to be distributed to his executioners, reminds us that His life was laid down for others and in implementation of His words to "pray for those who persecute you" (Matthew 5:44 RSV).

The main garment was made without a seam and this has come to mean that men belong to each other—that we cannot tear our corporate fabric apart without the destruction of our own inner selves.

In James Michener's story about Hawaii, the missionaries thought they were taking the good news westward when they set about introducing the whole bag of western-style living —even to the extent of trying to persuade these happy islanders to wear underwear. But that's not what the theology of clothes is all about. Clothes point to an inward spirit.

If the seamless robe is worth remembering, it is in order that we might remember the One who wore it and called men to behave like children of God.

"Say on, Demetrius!" said Gallio, thumping his desk impatiently.

"This Jesus of Galilee wore a simple, brown, homespun Robe to the cross. They stripped it off and flung it on the ground. While he hung there, dying, my master and a few other officers sat near-by playing with dice. One took up this Robe and they cast for it. My master won it. Later in the evening, there was a banquet at the Insula. Everyone had been drinking. . . . A Centurion urged my master to put on the Robe."

"Shocking idea!" grumbled Gallio. "Did he do it?"

"He did it—quite unwillingly. He had been very far gone in wine, in the afternoon, but was not steadied. I think he might have recovered from the crucifixion horror if it had not been for the Robe. He put it on—*and he has never been the same since!*"

"You think the Robe is haunted, I suppose." Gallio's tone was almost contemptuous.

"I think something happened to my master when he put it on. . . ."

The church is a fitting room. It is where we, too, slip our arms into the sleeves, pull its coarse cloth about our shoulders, and hurry out the door.

11
The Hidden Person

Becoming human involves exposing yourself to another person, letting someone see you as you really are, letting them touch and shape you at the core. Surely love has to do with that kind of closeness, that willingness to become vulnerable to another. I am intrigued by certain of Michaelangelo's statues in which only a portion of a man has been set free from the marble—a torso, a leg, an arm, the hint of a face—and the rest seems to be straining to break out of that stone prison. When I look at those partial figures they stir up in me a deep, deep longing to be completed, an ache to be set free from that which distorts and disguises, imprisons and inhibits my humanness, my wholeness. But as with those statues, I cannot liberate myself. For that I need the hand of another, the heart of another. Love, then, has to do with opening yourself to that other hand, that other heart. It has to do with receiving! It is difficult!

—THEODORE LODER

The most beautiful words in the Bible addressed to women are in the First Letter of Peter:

> Let not yours be the outward adorning with braiding of hair, decoration of gold, and wearing of robes, but let it be the hidden person of the heart with the imperishable jewel of a gentle and quiet spirit, which in God's sight is very precious. [3:3,4 RSV]

These words describe inward beauty. They speak of inward peace and a private self. Each of us, male and female, is an obvious, visible person. Each of us is also partly under canvas. We are not, however, hidden from God.

When Israel was trying to decide on a new king, after the death of Saul, the nation turned to the wisest man it knew, Samuel. And in making the choice, Samuel thought he knew. When an attractive young leader by the name of Eliab stood before him, Samuel, with his horn of oil, was ready to make the official pronouncement. In that moment, though, he heard God's voice: "Do not look on his appearance or on the height of his stature, because I have rejected him... the Lord sees not as man sees; man looks on the outward appearance, but the Lord looks on the heart" (1 Samuel 16:7 RSV).

The new king turned out to be, not Eliab, but David.

Is the hidden person of the heart the eye of a hurricane or a lagoon made for drifting boats, sparkling stars, and the sound of mandolins?

It can be either.

Our subterranean selves can be little knots of fear, cowards, bottled-up lust, just plain anger. Or they can be like a good friend who listens more than he talks or like a quiet garden or a Spanish monastery with old benches and rich combinations of sunlight and shade.

A man is not what he thinks he is, but what he *thinks,* he is.

We occasionally say of a person: "He's the kind of a guy who keeps things to himself." But that's almost certain to be inaccurate. There may be certain data—specific items of information—we can keep concealed from the world at large, but our feelings of love, of acceptance, of sympathy, like other feelings of guilt or hostility won't stay behind anybody's walls. We can't monitor our feelings and let only those show that we would like to have show. This is a little frightening to think about—to know that we stand as emotionally naked as we do in the presence of others. But it can also be liberating. It can be the signal to stop pretending. If people are going to know anyway what we really are, we might as well enjoy ourselves.

Inward beauty and inward freedom are first cousins. Beauty is a by-product of natural grace and freedom from pretense. It is swinging with the universe. It is Mary Martin crowing when she wants to crow. It is a thoroughbred running, birds flying, fish swimming, man laughing and loving.

These "hidden persons" stop being hidden when we unite them and let them go.

David Reisman's book *The Lonely Crowd* was about the

tragedy of hiddenness. And so is this poem by someone young:

> How absurd
> To be different
> From the crowd.
> Not too loud,
> Not too flashy.
> Not too brashy.
> Keep it cool,
> Not too mousy,
> Not a creep
> But not too neat.
> Take your cue from the
> Way they're talking—
> Way they're walking.
> Think like they think,
> Don't stand out.
> Don't be a square
> Nor too long hair.
> Play it safe man.
> Take it easy,
> Incoherent and even breezy
> Don't take the rap,
> And all that crap.
> Who wants to lead
> And maybe bleed?
> Don't stick your neck out,
>   Silly Boy
> Then you'll know
> That blissful joy
> Of never knowing who you are
> Or why you came, and
> Everyone can be the same—
> Without a name.

This makes us think of the fictional immortal Willy Loman, of whom his family said, in those last melancholy lines of *Death of a Salesman*, "He never knew who he was."

Learning to reveal our feelings is part of the trick of getting to know who we are. By the time we reach maturity as persons we wind up with several coats of varnish over our hearts. We are told more things we shouldn't do than things we should, and the true color of our lives tends to become lost. Our flow of blood slows down. We become guarded, suspicious, unsure. We become involved in the premeditated murder of ourselves. We become afraid of this inward person. We are afraid that when he tears his mask off he will look, more like Genghis Khan than God.

If the counterculture has occasionally expressed itself as incarnate irresponsibility, it has also taught, or at least asked, the straight world to go out again and experience what it feels like to yell across a meadow or forget about a clock.

Spontaneity of life. Perhaps even spontaneous combustion in which an old self we have lived with explodes in flame, and becomes ashes, and then vanishes, making way for a new person to be born.

This quality—this openness, this free spirit, this eloquence produced by a more unpremeditated style of life—is not only spontaneous; it is sensitive. It cares. Its receiver is on. It is listening for the pain-sounds of other people trying to break out of their shells. It listens for the cry of those who cannot say it but want to be noticed, want to be taken seriously, want to be loved.

Sensitivity to the thunder of the sea and the patience of the mountains spill over and become, or is part of, the business of being sensitive to persons.

Jesse Stuart wrote:

> Hold on to April; never let her pass!
> Another year before she comes again
> To bring us wind as clean as polished glass
> And apple blossoms in soft, silver rain.
> Hold April when there's music in the air,
> When life is resurrected like a dream,

> When wild birds sing up flights of windy stair
> And bees love alder blossoms by the stream.
> Hold April's face close yours and look afar,
> Hold April in your arms in dear romance;
> While holding her look to the sun and star
> And with her in her faerie dreamland dance.
> Do not let April go but hold her tight.
> Month of eternal beauty and delight.

Jesus said, but probably didn't bother to write it down: "Let us love one another; for love is of God, and he who loves is born of God and knows God" (1 John 4:7 RSV).

No message of Christianity is plainer. To love God is not to love an idea in a vacuum; it is to love God *through people*. People "who need people are the luckiest people in the world" because God is as close as that.

Marian Chaplin, a composer who spends half of her time in the Bluegrass country and the other half on Sanibel Island off Florida's west coast, wrote about walking one morning along the Sanibel beach in a dense fog. She said she thought she was by herself until a sudden, hot shaft of sun consumed the fog-blanket in a matter of seconds. As she looked around, she noticed quite a number of other people nearby.

Life, by its pressure to be efficient and socially cooperative, forces upon us a certain flatness—deadness of soul, unawareness, banality of being. A businessman at lunch might be heard saying: "I have to go now, Jim; I'll pay the bill to the waitress. . . . Well, hello, Jerry. It's been a long time since we've met in town. How's Janet? . . . You were divorced last year? I didn't know that. I'm sorry. Oh, Jim, have you got change for the tip? Goodby, Jerry. . . . Ready, Jim, I want to pick up a paper. I'm worried about the weather for a party we're having tomorrow night. Look at these headlines! War in Angola again. Oops—pardon me, fellow. . . . What's that? . . . No, there is a Perkins Street about four blocks from here, but I've never heard of Perdue Street. . . ."

We are also reluctant to care—not only because we become too involved in the hurly-burly of a push-button civilization, but because caring exposes us so often to hurt. Caring is usually a mixture of joy and suffering. Still it is the main door into the real world. Until we have walked through it, we haven't really seen the face of God.

Caring is dangerous, wrote a high-school girl:

> It leaves you open to hurt and to looking a fool; and perhaps it is because they have been hurt so often that people are afraid to care. I have found many places in my own life where I keep a secret store of indifference as a sort of self-protection, but I have been trying instead to feel the wholeness of the part and not shut myself up to life ... It's a hard thing and I have often failed.

Two handles to grab hold of, and both begin with *s:* spontaneity and sensitivity. Spontaneity—the freedom to be, the knocking down of walls blocking out what someone else will think. Sensitivity—the dignity and delight, yes, the divine element, involved in caring a heaven of a lot about other people.

Love is the meaning of life, and love is caring. In Jesus, God lays down His life for us.

Add serenity.

"God grant me the serenity to accept things I cannot change, courage to change things I can, and wisdom to know the difference."

The hidden person can be a center of calm rather than of chaos. The Spirit of God can preempt our spirit—taking from us the spirit of confusion and disorder, frenzy and fear, and replacing it with the confidence that God's will is unfolding in ways that surpass our understanding.

We need to handle life with a light touch because it is not ours to keep. It is ours to use. We have to release our grip on our possessions, on the lives of those we love, even on ourselves. We cannot be free unless we do. And this hidden person we have been describing will stay a stranger.

We were made for a bigger room than Earth. We are not

animals biting each other and crawling about in the selfish brush for 70 years, then turning back into fertilizer. We are the children of God. Our lives are tinted with immortality from the day we are born!

I once took a snapshot of our two younger children as they stood pensively in front of the Lion of Lucerne in Switzerland. When the picture was developed, it had an unexpected charm. Just as the lens opened, a pigeon waddled onto the scene. In the photograph he is sitting there, watching the children watch the lion. Similarly did a dove once look down upon the baptism of a brave-eyed Jew.

"The hidden person . . . the imperishable jewel of a gentle and quiet spirit . . ." The poise that comes through prayer; the peace that comes through prayer; the peace that comes through faith; the hope that comes through trusting the Father of all mercies, the God of all comfort; the strength that comes through waiting for God's plans to reach completion —it is the part of us, put there by God, that belongs in a special way to Him. It is that restive intangible that wants to be more than it is, that cries out within us for expression, freedom, love, joy, unity, fulfillment in nothing less than God himself.

Archaeologist Loren Eiseley, whose books say so much not just about the history of man and the universe but also the spiritual mystique that links us with the stars, describes an experience he once had with a small male hawk he had captured for purposes of scientific study.

He found some birds in an abandoned mountain cabin and was sorry not to be able to catch a pair to study, but the female got away. He put him in a small box for the night. The next morning he brought the box out onto the grass with the idea of making a cage. He looked up into the deep blue of the sky to see if there was any sign of the other little hawk but she had evidently gone for good.

Eiseley describes what happened next:

> Secretively, I looked again all around the camp and up and down and opened the box. I got him right out

in my hand with his wings folded properly and I was careful not to startle him. He lay limp in my grasp and I could feel his heart pound under the feathers but he only looked beyond me and up.

I saw him look that last look away beyond me into a sky so full of light that I could not follow his gaze. The little breeze flowed over me again, and nearby a mountain aspen shook all its tiny leaves. I suppose I must have had an idea then of what I was going to do, but I never let it come up into consciousness. I just reached over and laid the hawk on the grass.

He lay there a long minute without hope, unmoving, his eyes still fixed on that blue vault above him. It must have been that he was already so far away in heart that he never felt the release from my hand. He never even stood. He just lay with his breast against the grass.

In the next second after that long minute he was gone. Like a flicker of light, he had vanished with my eyes full on him, but without actually seeing even a premonitory wing beat. He was gone straight into that towering emptiness of light and crystal that my eyes could scarcely bear to penetrate. For another long moment there was silence. I could not see him. The light was too intense. Then from far up somewhere a cry came ringing down.

I was young then and had seen little of the world, but when I heard that cry my heart turned over. It was not the cry of the hawk I had captured; for, by shifting my position against the sun, I was now seeing further up. Straight out of the sun's eye, where she must have been soaring restlessly above us for untold hours, hurtled his mate. And from far up, ringing from peak to peak of the summits over us, came a cry of such unutterable and ecstatic joy that it sounds down across the years and tingles among the cups on my quiet breakfast table.

The hidden person of the heart. Where eloquence is born.

12
If There Is a Holy Spirit—

> If there is a holy spirit,
> If there is a heavenly dove,
> I would like to see and hear it,
> Changing this cold world with love.
>
> —FOLK HYMN

This song reminds us of Paul's experience at Ephesus where he met some new Christians and inquired if they had received the Holy Spirit. They answered, with priceless honesty, "We haven't even heard that there *is* a Holy Spirit!" Luke says they were baptized—this time in the name of Jesus—and that they were filled with the enthusiasm of the new faith.

Though the words Holy Spirit continue to be prominent in the language of our worship, we remain confused about their meaning.

It does not satisfy most of us to think of the Holy Spirit in terms of speaking in tongues or testifying in public about our conversion. Still, we affirm the Spirit. We know that, unless we have the Spirit of God, or the Spirit has us, we are merely playing games—perhaps even wasting time on weekends when we *could* be out tromping the beaches or doing other happy things to wash the tension out of our bodies and shoddy thoughts out of our minds.

What is the Holy Spirit?

In a sermon in a rural church in eastern Kentucky I once made reference to the Holy Spirit. I spoke about the Spirit as the gift of God, as an energy of love and faith. I said that when we receive the Holy Spirit we look out upon the world through new eyes. We see Christ in the faces of our fellowmen. We become witnesses to a Power that is expressing itself through us.

Afterward, the Lincolnesque pastor of the parish, Sam Vandermeer, came up and said: "That was a fine sermon, but why did you not refer to the Holy Spirit as 'He'? The Spirit is a Person." Driving home, I recalled the words of the majestic hymn "Holy, Holy, Holy" and its statement concerning deity: "God in Three Persons, blessed Trinity!" I wondered about Sam's question—all the way back to Lexington. Why did it seem unnatural to me to refer to the Holy Spirit as "He"? It sounded like a fairly basic point.

> If there is a holy spirit,
> If there is a heavenly dove . . .

"We have never even heard there is a Holy Spirit!"

Let's disabuse ourselves of the idea that there is a nice, neat theological explanation which, if we could get our hands upon it, would straighten out all our confusion.

If we look at the Bible as a whole, we see the Spirit referred to in many ways. Sometimes it (He) comes "upon men." Other times it (He) "fills" them.

Ezekiel writes of one of his encounters with God. "Then a spirit lifted me up, and I heard behind me a fierce rushing sound as the glory of the Lord rose from his place. I heard the sound of the living creatures' wings brushing against one another" (Ezekiel 3:12 NEB).

The Spirit speaks, is poured out, causes "old men to dream dreams, and young men to see visions."

When Jesus is baptized at the Jordan, the Spirit "descends like a dove." In John's Gospel, in a description of one of the resurrection appearances, Jesus appears to the disciples who are huddled behind locked doors. He says: "Peace be with you! As the Father has sent me, even so I send you." Then, says the writer, "he breathed on them, and said to them, 'Receive the Holy Spirit' " (20:21, 22 RSV).

In The Acts of the Apostles, the Holy Spirit comes and men begin to speak in different languages. God is glorified through this outpouring, and the church filled with fresh life and promise.

If you're confused about the Holy Spirit, join the club!

At the same moment we admit that here is something that is as hard to understand as death, we admit that what we have under discussion is as basic as God.

The Holy Spirit, in part, at least, is the God-quality in our lives. It is the quality of hope in a pessimistic age. To live a life of hope is something. Hope is different from wishful thinking. It is different from optimism. It is "not belief in spite of evidence, but life in scorn of consequence."

The Holy Spirit is the quality of love in a time of war.

It is the passion for justice which burns fiercely in the soul and bloodstream of a few.

It is the freedom that stands in opposition to certain other qualities which also make up what we are: fear, uptightness, neurosis.

The Holy Spirit is the quality of generosity, our devotion to Truth.

It is the quality that stands in contradiction to sin, greed, envy, spite, jealousy, lust, cruelty.

The Holy Spirit may show up in our lives in dramatic ways, but it is neither limited nor even experienced primarily in church buildings or in church services.

The Holy Spirit is converted human spirit.

"The spirit of man is the candle of the Lord."

The Holy Spirit and human spirit are as interrelated as heat and light are to the activity of the sun.

I remember my first trip home after my mother died. The

furniture was there. Dad was there. There was food in the cupboards and the pictures were still on the walls, but the spirit of the home was gone; it had flown away.

Each autumn we get a taste of the spirit of Notre Dame as the Irish topple one football opponent after another.

In California we experience the spirit of the West, a carryover of the frontier.

In Henry Miller's introduction to a book on Beniamino Bufano, the San Francisco sculptor who died in 1970, there is mention of the spirit of Japan. Japanese art, says Miller, involves itself in everything the Japanese do. It permeates the total Japanese culture, the whole business of living, which in America tends to be utilitarian. Yankees are more concerned with results than with esthetics, which is the spirit of Eastern civilization.

The most serious problem in American society now is not a lack of esthetic sensitivity but a lack of will. America's present crisis is a crisis of desire. We have the tools, skills, resources to do whatever we want to do, build what we want to build, be what we want to be. But what we want is unclear. We don't know what we want to become or what is even worth becoming. It is the spirit of America, even more than the economy, which is in need of rescue.

The God-quality is what the late Donald Baillie said was total in Jesus but fragmentary and sporadic in us. Dr. Baillie said that is what the incarnation means, why we can speak of Jesus as God's self-disclosure. God in Man—faith, hope and love in completeness of expression, and in human packaging.

But the Holy Spirit is more than all this. The Holy Spirit is God—*God present* within our experience.

To think of or speak of the Holy Spirit as "He" or "Him" is to protect our minds from false notions about "where" God is, or how His life impinges upon our own.

To speak of God as Heavenly Father is easy for us. It is natural. It gives us the feeling we belong. It is our way of saying we belong to Meaning, that we belong to a Family, that we stand in the shadow of a wise Parent whose love and protection and wisdom is greater than our own. But this image for all of its beauty and accuracy may still leave us with the feeling of someone who stands at a distance, who cares for us, yes, but from a far-off "fatherly" headquarters. After all, we do not live our lives in the presence of our fathers. We get bounced on their knees, we get scolded and soothed by them. Then we say good-bye, head out into the world.

To "image" God as Jesus is also an important part of our knowledge of who God is, what He is like, how He reacts to us when we fail, what He hopes we can, in freedom, become. But Jesus is part of history. He lived in a different time than our own. He never saw an airplane, a typewriter, or an electric light. We can love Jesus, but, again, there is the problem of distance—this time historical distance.

When we begin to speak of God as Holy Spirit, there is no distance. The Holy Spirit means God is present in everything that happens to us. He meets us in our prayer life, in our struggles, our friendships, our decisions; He is present in the naked, the sick, and the poor. The Holy Spirit allows God to be God, the God of the next two minutes, the God we cannot escape, who never deserts us even when we are hanging on the cross of life.

Ray Swartzback, campus Minister at the College of Wooster, puts it with similar marksmanship:

> We have been so busy merchandising the church's old religious goods, dressing them up to sell better, that we have neglected the scandal of the gospel— neglected to say it in unmistakably clear language that it was and is in flesh and in community, with all the stresses and crises, that man has his transcendent nature revealed to him.

Our transcendent nature is revealed to us through all our secular meetings. Our spirit and God's spirit touch at both plain and surprising points and there is lightning. Renewal and rebirth.

The Holy Spirit is like a drop of dew the sunlight hits and

turns into seven colors. The Holy Spirit is God refusing to accommodate Himself to our little intellectual categories; it is God overrunning them, ignoring them, consuming them.

We are only able to speak of God in parables, for God is love, and love can never be explained. We can only say it is like this or like this or like this. Hope can't be explained, either, or heaven, or even forgiveness.

In Ingmar Bergman's film *The Silence* a young woman, in an overnight stop in a city gives herself to casual sex for money and is dumped into a pit of self-loathing and guilt. As she continues on her journey in a train, with her little boy at her side, a storm drenches the countryside with rain. Impulsively, the window is thrown open. The rain, the wind beat into her face, soaking her as she gropes for cleansing in the fresh, clean water.

In our lives, in the most ordinary circumstances, we have had glimpses of God, experiences of His comfort and help, intimations of His displeasure. We have tried to write about them, tried to talk about them, for such moments reach deep into the secret of self as well as into the heart of the universe. But God is greater than words, so our theology of the Holy Spirit comes out disconnected and confused.

An ad in the *Los Angeles Times* evokes a mixture of sympathy and resented exploitation. It says: "For instructions in a new quick easy way to receive the Holy Ghost, check this box, and mail with 50¢"

Jesus puts it better in his conversation with Nicodemus: "The wind blows where it wills; you hear the sound of it, but you do not know where it comes from, or where it is going. So with everyone who is born from spirit" (John 3:8 NEB).

We cannot control these tradewinds of God, these Santa Anas of the soul. God will not allow Himself to be confined to our convenience, nor can we ever know for sure just where, and in what ways, God is most pointedly at work. If we cannot control them, we can open our lives to their cleansing and invigorating power.

We are better off trying to follow Jesus the best we can in our daily lives, keeping open to God's intrusions whatever they may be and leaving alone the mystery of whether we "have" the Holy Spirit or "don't have" it (I mean Him!).

If someone asks me if I am a twice-born Christian, I feel like answering, "Well, what do you think?"

Let God judge—or, at the least, the people who know us, see us, hear us, feel the force of our lives. Maybe, even though they don't get around to putting it into words, they may reach some silent conclusion such as this one by Frank Whitney:

> I behold the Christ in you
> > Here the life of God I see
> I can see a great peace, too,
> > I can see you whole and free.
>
> I behold the Christ in you
> > I can see this as you walk
> I see this in all you do
> > I can see this as you talk.
>
> I behold God's love expressed
> > I can see you filled with power
> I can see you ever blessed
> > See Christ in you, hour by hour.
>
> I behold the Christ in you.
> > I can see that perfect one
> Led by God in all you do
> > I can see God's work is done.

The "if" of the folk hymn denotes contingency: "*If* there is a holy spirit, *If* there is a heavenly dove, . . ." The "if" can go. There *is* a Holy Spirit. He is God, knocking on the door of our lives—God offering us a new chance, calling to us to join with Him in work and justice and peace.

One word will do for a response: Yes.

IV
HE AIN'T HEAVY FATHER; HE'S MY BROTHER

13
Theodore Hesburgh Skins Our Eyes

Our day is but a gleam of light between two nights of dark. The mists hang about our minds, our feet are fettered, we are bruised and bound, robbed and cheated every day. Yet we can conceive a higher knowledge beside which ours is poor and incomplete. Though our ignorance is well-nigh universal, at least we know we do not know; our night is never so long or so dark that we forget what the day is like. Yet we are more than we seem, and Thou art nearer than we dream. We only dare to ask for light upon one step ahead, faith to take one day at a time, endurance to wait for the dawn. Forgive us, O Father, the crushing care that comes from our lack of vision.

—W. E. ORCHARD

One of the best lines of the Old Testament is from Proverbs: "Where there is no vision, the people perish" (29:18 KJV). That same sentence in the Revised Standard Version reads: "Where there is no prophecy the people cast off restraint." Either way, the principle fits the times.

Father Theodore Hesburgh, president of the University of Notre Dame, and a giant among college presidents, evoked a cry of "Thank God!" when he came out a few years ago for a tougher stand against the "trashing," burning, bombing, and intimidating tactics of campus radicals. Hesburgh has been one of the champions of the liberal spirit, believing universities must be both intellectually free and self-regulating if they are to be universities dedicated to truth and not the hired instruments of the state or some political faction.

Thus it was not only *what* was said but *who* said it that produced this burst of hope.

"Rational discussions and thoughtful attacks on the social concerns of our existence cannot be carried on," Hesburg said, "in a boiler factory." If demonstrators care about people and about finding answers to the problems people have, they will, said the president of Notre Dame, let these institutions get on with the job in some framework of freedom—freedom for the advocates of *all kinds* of proposals as to what is good for man and what it will take to create a world of peace with justice. Tolerance of ideas we do not agree with is the heart-muscle of democracy.

Father Hesburgh analyzed our situation in one compelling sentence: "The real crisis today is not one of authority; it is a crisis of vision."

"The real crisis is not one of authority. . . ."

It's not?

It surely looks like it!

Who's running the schools anyway? The administration or the students? Who's running the cities? The city council or the anarchists?

Who's running the family? Parents or children?

Who's running the Roman Catholic church? The Pope or the rebel priests?

There may be a crisis of authority, but it is rooted in a deeper crisis—an optical one. In business, a worker must be enabled to *see* the larger operation of which he is a part or he will be a dull, dissatisfied puppet. A graduate student loads on to himself long hours and hard work because he can *see* where he's headed and where he wants to get. In our family conflicts we say to each other, "I don't *see* why. . . ." And we don't and we stay frustrated and angry until we do.

Seeing is not believing. Believing is seeing. Seeing the image of God in Jesus of Nazareth. Seeing, in another person, beauty and possibility. When we cannot see or where there is no prophecy (life examined through the prism of faith), people cast off restraint and fall into the ditch of disorder.

The vision that can save us has three ingredients. They cannot be tackled piecemeal. Unless we are committed to all three, simultaneously, we will not succeed at any. They are law and order, justice in our times, and love between generations.

We are called by God to embrace them all, to consolidate them into a single unifying vision that can outdistance civil war.

To reach the moon, it took a booster rocket, a space capsule, and a lunar exploration module. These were interdependent parts of one program to land men on the moon. None could carry off the space conquest alone.

If we seek only law and order, we are doomed. Hitler's Germany, with its goose-stepping soldiers and precisely regulated society, was a master production so far as order was concerned. Every man knew what was expected of him and what all the prohibitions were. If a person violated any one of them or discussed them with his neighbor, he risked a two-o'clock-in-the-morning visit from the Gestapo.

Law and order is good politics. It sounds virtuous and desirable, and terribly, terribly welcome in a society that has known as much disrespect for authority as ours has.

And it *is* good if it remains yoked to other ideals for which hundreds of thousands of men have given two-thirds of their lives.

Law and order alone? No.

Justice, yes. The Old Testament shouts justice on every page. Jesus enters the scenario heralded by a preacher-baptizer who shouted to the leaders of his society: "You brood of vipers! Who warned you [Sadducees] to flee from the wrath to come? Bear fruit that befits repentance" (Matthew 3:7, 8 RSV).

But justice can't stand alone, either. Justice is not a textbook abstraction. You can stand on a street corner for ten years shouting justice. Justice for all! But if this is *all* you do, you only make a nuisance of yourself. Justice must be translated into pragmatic possibilities, into laws and budgets. Law is the instrument of justice, the servant of righteousness.

Justice cannot be achieved by tearing law fabric to shreds. Neither is it served by the clamor to silence those who protest things as they are. A man who is interested only in the security of his own existence is a democratic liability and a Christian tramp.

The Bible has too much to say about justice—especially for the poor, the homeless, the hungry, and the sick—to let our commitment to mind our own business suffice as our responsibility to peace. There are too many people in too much pain for that!

If dissent has produced great anxiety across the land, threatening the survival of the country, excess should not blind the nation to the reality that, at the center of the storm, stand a million young people who just may care more than some of the rest.

Some of their idealism is made out of clouds. Some get down to the nitty-gritty of things we could change in our society if we wanted to. We just don't want to. We like things the way they are.

Out of the knowledge that many of us World War II types are unwilling to change, grow, and revise comes the failure of both trust and love between generations. We have even begun to feel revulsion toward each other. Long hair on men produces instant alienation among traditionalists. They want no further relationships of any kind. All they can see and feel is defiance of what they themselves are. They are threatened. They know what is right. They know what is good, what is proper, what is decent. Don't try to change my ideas!

Those who live in the country of the young are trying to show us their vision of a new world. But they must bear their share of responsibility for love's failure. If oldsters often feel their scorn, the under-thirties must admit to close-mindedness, too. For all of their placarding of love, they have ignored love's first requirement: the readiness to listen to these voices of experience.

It is no answer to say "We've listened long enough."

The crisis of vision involves the need to see that law and order, justice in our times, and love between generations are three sides of one jewel.

We cannot love only law and order.

We cannot merely cry "justice" without taking into account how justice is translated from shouted slogans into legal fulfilment.

When a little boy misbehaved, his mother scolded him.

"Don't do that!" she scolded.

"Why not?" he inquired.

"Because I said so. And because I'm your mother. When I was a little girl, I had to do what my mother told me to do. And when she was little, she had to do what her mother told her."

The boy asked, "Who started it all, anyway?"

Ours is not a crisis of authority. It is not a matter of which side will prove strong enough to force the other to knuckle to its will. It is a crisis of vision which involves the readiness to see what the other man is driving at, plus a love which can enable people to understand how much they need each other in the attainment of common goals.

Leadership is vision. It is someone who sees possibilities and points them out.

Faith is vision. We do not die on the day of our death. We die that day when we give up the vision of something more we want to become.

Love is vision. Someone says of a certain man's attraction for a certain woman, "I don't know what he sees in her" or, conversely "I don't know what she sees in him." No, he doesn't. But the parties involved see what the rest of us do not. It's like the lyrics of Sheldon Harnick's song in *Fiddler on the Roof:*

> But of all God's miracles large and small
> The most miraculous one of all
> Is the one I thought could never be
> God has given you to me.

Peace is vision. Peace is movement—movement directed toward God and the good.

Many of us like the world very much as it is. I do. I grew up in a modest but beautiful home. I experienced no discrimination I can remember, though we lived near the railroad tracks. I have enjoyed political freedom. Good health. A good education. A good job. My children go to good schools. I have never experienced serious hunger.

But my world is a small fraction of the real world, and I need to understand that most of the world is not like mine. Although the world the way it is and America as it is suits me fine, there is a legion of the disenfranchised whom it does not satisfy. This must be part of the vision I live with. If I give it up, I am only half a man.

If we can see the problem, we can do something about it. Then we have at least some chance of loving each other and supporting each other while we hack away.

First, we must *see*. We must *see* the real dimensions of human despair. We must *see* each other as persons, not statistics. Seeing involves a whole series of Damascus Road encounters—receiving sight from the Physician who touched the eyes of the blind, who changed human forms from trees to faces.

The revolutionary counts on the blindness of the power structure. In Czarist Russia, while princes drank champagne in the Winter Palace, the leaders of the peasants had more than sugar plums dancing in their heads. The blindness of those in authority was quite necessary to the strategy of surprise.

There can be no eloquence without seeing how much distance remains between the dream with which our nation began and the millions who have not shared in it! No eloquence unless we seize, without self-pity, this three-part vision which can save us from dinosaurial death, from the melancholy extinction that awaits us if we decide we can't make the transition into the new age, the dawn of which is already lighting up the eastern sky.

Alfred McBride wrote in the June, 1969, issue of *The Pulpit:*

> Our situation today is explosive. The Vietnam war summons images of a third world war and of a bombing that will contaminate not just our milk but sear our lives and continents and the very health of children yet unborn. Automation glibly and sometimes cruelly robs thousands of unskilled workers of their jobs. The population explosion presents the picture of the sheer multiplicity of men depriving us not just of our privacy but even of space to live and a piece of bread to eat.
>
> But we also have a world of promise in which atomic energy will water deserts, computers will program living space and undreamed-of leisure possibilities. The Kingdom of God is a call to subdue the earth and enter with confidence into the world of the future with both its frightening promise of tragedy and its glorious pledge of new freedom and human development. I hope Christ will not weep over our generation. I hope you will not lament at the gate. This is a time of visitation. The disasters are the overturning of the old order. Be not blind. Do not refuse to change. Welcome the emerging world with joy, for, after all, it is God's world and He loves it.

Thanks, Father Hesburgh, for skinning our eyes!

14
Martin Luther King, Jr., and Robert Kennedy Return to Ask Some Questions

Whence rise you, Lights? From this tower built upon Manhattan's native rock. Its roots are deep below forgotten musket balls, the mouldered wooden shoe, the flint, the bone. What mark you, Lights? Our Nation's doorway. Who sleep or toil beneath your good warm gaze? All who love this Land: they who are of the Land's stout seed, and they who love the Land because they chose to come. Sing you a song, Proud Lights? We sing silently. We chant a Mass and Spiritual, Doxology and Kol Nidre, battle hymn and ballad. We tell of village and of jet—Of wheat and cotton, turbine, oil and goldenrod, the wildest mountains and the cities' roar. This is a strange new time, Strong Lights, why never do you fear? There is something more powerful, The heart and soul of all Mankind. What build you with your beams? A bridge to the stars. What offer you to God, O Lights? America's devotion.

—MACKINLAY KANTOR
(The Empire State Lights)

A great sadness swept over America in 1968 as a result of the assassinations of Martin Luther King, Jr., and Robert Francis Kennedy. There was a quality in their humanity, an optimism in their citizenship that enriched two hundred million lives.

They were Christian men.

They argued and struggled for the repair of the American family. The questions they raised with such insistency in the forums of public decision turned them into murderers' targets. Leaders who can convince deprived people that there exists an honest concern about them are men to be valued and remembered.

Kennedy exemplified a personal ruggedness, welcome in an age of softness.

King stood in the prophetic tradition of both the Old and New Testaments in a way that welded Moses and Mississippi into one reality.

The courage of the two families involved, in their turning to God in an hour of unbearable grief, sent the rest of us on inward journeys to see what resources *we* possess for the meeting of tragedy and pain. It takes greatness of spirit to sing Handel's Chorus while your heart is breaking. Still, that's what faith is about.

The irreplaceability of a human life is a staggering thought. It is partly alleviated by the Walter Scott poetic conclusion:

> Sound, sound the clarion, fill the fife!
> To all the sensual world proclaim,
> One crowded hour of glorious life
> Is worth an age without a name.

Following Robert Kennedy's death, newspaper editors tried to articulate the feeling of wounds retorn and shame compounded. One noted that the space between killings seemed to be shorter.

It is unfair to take these crimes and treat them as proof that the United States has demonstrated it is beyond all doubt an evil land made up of evil men. But there is enough connection between these crimes to make us tremble. Two deaths, two months apart, screamed a question. Who *does* speak for the country? What does America represent in the marketplace of values? Does she have anything to export that anybody else could possibly want? Where are we headed?

The time is overdue for return—or advance—to a society which is less cynical, less vulgar, less hedonistic, less permissive, less brutal, and less conceited. Today's huge interest in ecology is one form of appeal to a gentler version of living.

It is time to start erasing a reputation for violence we have earned by making it clear we are not willing to let our military presence in Asia, valiant or misguided, continue to substitute for international responsibility. We must find a better answer to the stewardship of American strength. Freedom is worth dying for, but only if, in our dying, we do not turn into a pack of wolves.

We cannot anticipate much improvement if we depend primarily on missile and antimissile systems to sustain us into the future. The world will not buy, nor honor, our dream on these grounds. We must be more than birdmen or chemists. If man were simply hamburger or an arrangement of circuits, we could forget moral criteria. But, as Abraham J. Heschel said, "Humanity without divinity is a torso." We cannot keep a nation alive with dead men.

Peace does not mean merely the absence of conflict. It means something affirmative, something aggressive.

A man who has enjoyed his work and been productive and then is thrust into effortless retirement with no more battles to fight, no more tough decisions to make, no business to worry about is usually not at peace. He must find new challenges and enterprises and sacrifices to take the place of old ones or he finds himself living in hell.

Jesus did not understand peace in terms of an undisturbed teaching ministry in Alexandria but as a ride into Jerusalem on a mule.

Violence corrupts humanity.

So does silence. The "silent majority" may be the "chicken majority."

We have witnessed riots and burnings and lootings. But there are other forms of violence, too, which need to be resisted. There is a way of looking at the American scene which involves the notion that all people who raise questions, create division, or challenge authority are troublemakers and disturbers of the peace. This can turn out to be a pious avoidance of other violences we do not want to look in the eye because they are not the kind that threaten *us*.

Violence is involved in allowing human beings to be destroyed if it is in our power to change things. Not the overt violence of a bullet fired into someone else's brain but, rather, the violence of violation—the violation of one's humanity. When people are destroyed at the same time it is within our capacity to help them, we are not inclined to call it violence. But those who are on the dirty end of the stick call it that in their bones. That's why their retaliations do not bother them. The secure worry about gasoline bombs because they have much to lose. Many others do not.

Who have been the most moral men in our times? Were the youngsters who began the sit-ins and joined the freedom rides and defied the dogs and went to jail the trouble causers? Shall we look at our torn-up society and say, "That's where it began"? Or were *they* the moral ones, rather than those who, without indignation, didn't bother to get into the fight? We are opposed to violence. But are we opposed only on our terms?

The rebuilding of American unity and confidence must occur on many fronts. At some time the people of the United States must decide to deal seriously with the Kerner report.

Another issue involves recovery of the feeling that individual men count and are not lost in mass organization.

One of the reasons we felt such keen losses in the deaths of King and Kennedy is because they were distinctive men. Mass structures not only crucify our souls; they also become hiding places. The nonviolent men we aspire to be must be men who have the nerve to step out of the crowd and announce who they are.

Jesus is our key to authentic manhood. No social program, however well conceived or financed, can make a man a man. We can put a gorilla into a four-bedroom home with an all-electric kitchen and a swimming pool, but that does not make him a man. It takes God at work in a man's life to do that.

Who can forget this paragraph from *Dr. Zhivago:*

Rome was a flea market of borrowed gods and conquered peoples, a bargain basement on two floors, earth and heaven, a mass of filth convoluted in a triple knot as in an intestinal obstruction. Dacians, Herulians, Scythians, Samaritans, Hyperboreans, heavy wheels without spokes, eyes sunk in fat, sodomy, double chins, illiterate emperors, fish fed on the flesh of learned slaves . . . all crammed into the passages of the Coliseum and all wretched.

And then, into this tasteless heap of gold and marble, He came, light and clothed in an aura, emphatically human, deliberately provincial, Galilean, and at that moment gods and nations ceased to be and man came into being—man the carpenter, man the plowman, man the shepherd with his flock of sheep at sunset, man who does not sound in the least proud, man thankfully celebrated in all the cradle songs of mothers and in all the picture galleries the world over.

Let Christians celebrate this potential to do the will of God! Thus will the angers and estrangements that killed King and Kennedy be energies of a brighter decade.

15
Whatever Is Necessary to Get My People Out of Hell

The Church has always been called upon to make known the good news, to pray for those who cannot pray, to love

those who are not loved, to speak courageously on behalf of those who are silent, to teach the young, to bury the dead, to work as a catalyst for peace and reconciliation, i.e., never to accept a word of hatred or discrimination or despair, as a final word of man's situation. This is not new, or, to put it more precisely, although it is not "new" in the sense of a historically or sociologically definable new situation, it always "becomes new" when it happens. Love is "new" in a situation of hate, and so is the courage to speak words of life at a time of death. . . .
—DIETRICH RITSCHL

I've never visited Fresno, though, in the course of trips to northern California, I've made stops there for gasoline. One day when I stopped there the temperature was 105°.

In the spring of 1969 a black militant by the name of Marvin Jackmon continued to teach classes at Fresno State College in spite of the fact that he had been ordered not to do so by the chancellor. A news story which came out of that gesture of defiance included the toughest of all questions in Christian ethics. Said this angry American, "I am ready to do whatever is necessary to get my people out of hell."

This apparently means that the goal he has in mind is so important he will use any means available—*any means*—to see it realized. If nonviolent methods are ineffective, violence it will have to be.

We could say: How can there be any doubt about the wrongness of that viewpoint? Is not violence *always* a contradiction to the teachings of Christianity? Did not Jesus command us to love even enemies, to turn the other cheek? And there are the words from the cross: "Father, forgive them; for they know not what they do."

"I am ready to do whatever is necessary to get my people out of hell."

This is not one lonely voice. It is many voices. And not only the voices of blacks. It is increasingly the posture of the young who insist they are determined to overhaul the system.

This is threatening to almost everyone born before World War II. We are inclined to react by saying that this is the cry of anarchy—that it contradicts everything we understand about decent relationships between people, everything we understand about constitutional democracy, everything we understand about religion, and the civilized values of rational thought. There is no way to make a valid case for violence. Even when things are terrible, violence is not justifiable because violence breeds violence. It violates the laws of God. It violates the laws of humanity.

How, then, can we talk about this being a "tough question"? If all this is so, the question is answered. It is no longer a question.

But it *is* a question. It will remain a question forever.

It will remain a question because there are things men care deeply about. This is part of our humanity, too. If we didn't care so much about them, we could say to Mr. Jackmon: The most important thing for *you* to be concerned about is not getting your people out of hell, but preserving the American system, or using only those means to achieve your goal that are lawful and not destructive of the larger human commonwealth.

If we didn't care so much we could say that. But we do. If immoral means to achieve moral ends are *always* wrong—and they may be—if they are categorically ruled out, then American participation in all wars is and has been a fundamental mistake. For us to maintain a Department of Defense is a mistake. If we read the Sermon on the Mount carefully, there is no room for armed resistance. If we take the position, as many of us do, that there are *some* situations in which retaliation is justified—for example, if one has to kill a berserk person to save the life of his child—if self-defense is at least *one* exception to the canon that violence is always wrong, the fat is in the fire. At the least, we are left with the problem of deciding what constitutes legitimate self-defense.

"I am ready to do whatever is necessary. . . ."

If, on the lips of a Panther, those words sound frightening, on the lips of a young Czechoslovakian patriot, who says he, too, is ready to pay *any* price for freedom, they sound brave and representative of something precious among the spiritual treasures of man.

Is freedom so important we will risk the stigma of killing the few who would suppress it in order to save it for the many? About half of the people of the United States have taken the position that involvement in Indochina has had some justification in the light of the future of freedom. Freedom and survival both seem to be values so important we will aim guns and throw bombs to keep them from being taken away.

This may be the point at which you get off. You may be ready to say: I will not kill. There is no way to fight evil with evil.

For others, who also claim to love God, conscience and a concern for foreseeable consequences dictate a fight-to-the-death resistance.

Many who feel this way about freedom and a duty to die, if they must, to keep it alive still may have trouble agreeing with Jackmon that he's willing to dirty his hands by killing to win a battle that is just as important to him. In that case, Jackmon might turn upon them and say, "I thought *you* were talking about freedom as an exception. Man, this *is* freedom for me."

It's hard to get inside another man's skin. Most black people would be inclined to say that the white man tried but didn't make it, and that it's clear by now that he's never going to make it.

If there is hope for national reconciliation, it must lie in the determination of white people to keep on trying to feel some of the anguish, hurt, injury, bleeding that has been going on within black people for so long.

For four years I lived near the UCLA campus in West Los Angeles. Those were the same four years Lew Alcindor played college basketball there. In interviews, Lew often appeared sullen, alienated by his own choice. Once he made the remark, "This is not my country." Sports fans were proud, but found themselves feeling far away from him. They claimed him. They wanted him to claim them.

Just after the end of Alcindor's illustrious college career, *Sports Illustrated* published a story that made his negative spirit easier to understand. In a game he played as a highschooler, the coach chewed out Lew's team at half time for not giving a better account of themselves on the floor. Accusing them of laziness and nonalertness, he said at one point, "You played like a bunch of niggers." Alcindor said he would never forget that. Later the coach tried to pass it off as a shock-value joke. But the wound has stayed unhealed.

"I will do whatever is necessary to get my people out of hell."

If it's hard for Caucasians to feel the raw depths of those emotions, it is also hard to appreciate some other battles people are fighting.

If we have reasonably good health, a job, a place to live, friends, and are able to give our children most of the things they need to be well and happy, we are inclined to say: Don't rain on my parade. Our tolerance for the tactics of others striving to reach their goals is low. It's not our fight. We feel no desperation. We are willing for the fight to go on, but only so long as it doesn't knock holes in the bottom of our boat.

When it does become our fight, our cause, then our notions about what means are justified in order to win are going to change. We may begin feeling very mildly about a particular problem. Once we get into it, and begin to care a great deal about success or failure, our methodologies widen.

A risk suburbanites run is of being so well removed and protected from such struggles that they become overly critical of how they are being fought. We will go on being critical until, at some point, these wars become our own.

Twenty-five years ago a contract was let by the Iowa State Highway Commission to widen Highway 92 which runs through the middle of a community called Oskaloosa. That would sound, in many ways, like a good idea—a beautiful, wide new street. The problem lay in the tall, handsome oak trees which lined the thoroughfare from one end of town to the other and which had to be removed to make room for the new road. The morning the bulldozers fired up, ready to go to work removing the trees, residents came out of their homes and made human chains around the trees. The trees are still there.

Today, teachers and nurses strike on behalf of their professional objectives, actions which would have been rejected absolutely less than ten years ago.

What means are justified by what goals? It's a tough question. It was the heart of the Green Beret controversy. How important is national security? What price will we pay for it?

Californians remember with uneasy ambivalence what happened to American citizens of Japanese ancestry in 1942. The goal was correct. But did the urgency of the goal authorize the methods which were used to help us reach it?

A hundred fifty thousand General Electric workers went on strike. Families were faced with hardship; the company suffered, and the American economy suffered. Was the goal worth it? A vote was taken and, if the vote was honest, the opinion of the workers was yes.

In Rome bishops challenge the power of the papacy. One way of looking at their effort, which has brought surprising results, would be to say that the bishops are acting contentiously, that they are upsetting the church. Instead of helping the church achieve peace within its own life, they are feeding and enlarging the dissension. Another way of looking at that same set of circumstances would be to say that the goal is basic; it is right; it is essential to the church's integrity. Whatever the price is in terms of internal anxiety and confusion, it must be paid.

Violence in America will be with us for a long time. Most of us have children and grandchildren and we have thoughts of them as we try to answer the question of how to build, how to plan, how to change our social situation in such a way that they will not inherit a land of bloodshed and fear.

The Holy Spirit may be saying something like this: It is not enough to argue that violence is unacceptable. It *is* evil and unacceptable. That is Mr. Jackmon's point, and it is a valid point, whether uttered by a militant or anyone else. But there are more ways than one of killing as Jesus makes clear in The Sermon on the Mount. What we, who are seemingly secure, need to understand is that when counteractive violence occurs, it usually takes root in a violence already on the scene.

We should protest the breaking of laws if, at the same time, we protest conditions which sometimes—not always, but sometimes—lead men to break them.

In Connecticut, people broke laws which forbade the sale or distribution of birth-control devices and information. In Mississippi, liberals deliberately broke laws which forbade white and black people from riding together in taxicabs.

In 1776 American colonists deliberately refused to pay lawfully imposed taxes, then shot and slaughtered their way to a new condition of self-rule.

Means and ends—the toughest question of all. There's no book in which we can look to find infallible guidance. Christians read the same Bible and come forth with different understandings of how God would have us proceed.

There's a line in the Corinthian correspondence which might help. Paul is defending himself and his associates as trustworthy interpreters of the new truth which has come into the world in Jesus, "The love of Christ controls us" (2 Corinthians 5:14 RSV).

This may help determine which means are right in any particular situation.

Perhaps it's merely the business of trying to get along in the life of our families—trying to decide how, as young people, we can get our parents to understand us, or how, as parents, we can choose the path between overfirmness and overpermissive flabbiness.

A personal objective may help with the larger issues. It is to make the goals of full freedom and juster justice our own —then restudy the question of means in those terms.

Another is to know in our hearts that many of the questions

we are destined to live with are so massive they cannot be completely solved within our lifetimes. It is to know, too, that if our *means* are honorable and consistent with the ultimate goal, this may be the largest triumph of which we are capable.

There's an old saying: "There is no solution; seek it lovingly." We wind our way through an imperfect world. It is part of God's plan that we are never to be fully satisfied, the world never finished. We go seeking a city we can never find.

How we work away at the problem is the important thing. It is more important than finding the answers. If we must cheat our way to the top, it isn't worth getting there.

We can't kill our way to peace and freedom. Still, we can't let the freedom fire go out, or men rot in bondage and despair, while we thumb our handbooks on ethics.

Come, Lord Jesus, save us from ourselves!

16
Moonrocks Are Valuable, But So Are People

"What good is the moon?" People ask with an eye to the dollar. The scientists can only retort in answer "What good is a baby?"

—JEROME D. FRANK

Life began in the sea. How many millions or billions of years it took for life to move out of the salty waters onto the land, there to adapt itself to the nutrition of earth, rocks, air, and sunlight, we do not know. We do know that the results of that first leap onto the beach have proven interesting.

In our lifetime, the balance of being is shifting again. The life that came out of the oceans has demonstrated that it is bound for the stars. The doors of heaven are opening. Earth turns out to have been an overnight stop. The alarm has gone off. Another morning of our development has dawned. The endless journey goes on.

The moon landings almost defy the capacity of the intellect. The North American Rockwell Corporation's aviation division published a beautiful newspaper ad. The text said: "If you want some feeling of the immensity of the task represented by Apollo Eleven, walk out tonight under the stars and gaze upward. Then imagine, if the assignment were given to you, how or where you would begin."

Ten years ago our jaws dropped over the news that man had invented a basketball-sized satellite that could maintain perpetual orbit around the earth. Now we contemplate a grand tour observational visit of the planets in 1978 and manned landings on three or four before A.D. 2000.

Orville and Wilbur Wright's father was a minister who, it is reported, wasn't sure it was in God's plan that men should fly. Their mother, too, doubted the dream. "But God didn't give us wings!" she said laughingly, to them one day as they worked away on a strange-looking contraption in the backyard. Fortunately, these young men operated on the assumption that their dad had an expert knowledge of the Bible, but they had something he didn't: the first inkling of the mystery of aerodynamics.

The moon is a tiny coin of the universe, just as Earth is. Both say something eloquent about a purpose at the heart of things. They inspire us to raise questions about ourselves— to ask, and ask again: Who is Man?

Writes a poet-scientist:

> Out of the dreaming past, with its legends of steaming seas and gleaming glaciers, mountains that moved and suns that glared, emerges this creature,

man—the latest phase in a continuing process that stretches back to the beginning of life. His is the heritage of all that has lived; he still carries the vestiges of snout and fangs and claws of species long since vanished; he is the ancestor of all that is yet to come. Do not regard him lightly. He is you.

What more compelling word is there from God as to the meaning of the July 20, 1969, miracle—this escape from Earth Island—this first step in an adventure we know will carry our children to worlds beyond?

Is there more to say than "Gee Whiz"? Or "We certainly showed the Russians!" or "Where can you make reservations for Golden Coach service to the Sea of Tranquility?"

Listen: God has given man dominion over the Earth. "Thou hast put all things under his feet" (Psalms 8:6 RSV). Dominion sounds good. *Domino* means God. Dominion means power. Action power. Veto power. The power of choice and decision. The power to kill, the power to save. The power to create. The power to destroy. The power to say, *"Domino!"*

God has given man a fundamental quality of himself—the quality of *domino*. God, do You know what You are doing? Do You know what You've done? You could have managed things differently, but You didn't. You have given to man a share of responsibility for shaping Your ultimate dream, plus a Spirit against which to measure the correctness of our work. The late President John F. Kennedy had this truth in mind when he said, "In this world, the work of God must be our own."

There is a version of Christianity that shrinks from statements like that. It imagines itself to be honoring God by disclaiming responsibility for the world. It says man's role is inconsequential. God is running the universe. Man is a peanut. What does man have to say about the final outcome? This is God's world. He is the Executive Producer. The clay cannot tell the Potter what to do. Armageddon is approaching. Get down on your knees.

If that's "where it's at" for you, I probably cannot change your mind. Nor will I try very hard.

I will match that definition of loving God with another, one which says that God has put into the hands of man the job of "dominating" the world for good.

To be given dominion and, with dominion, responsibility for the results is not exactly an occasion for a fresh round of drinks. It is reason, rather, to pray, "God, for both Your sake and our own, help us, fill us with Holy Spirit, and show us patient mercy when we mess things up."

We made it to the moon. Great! Fantastic! Let's cry, feast, clap our hands that we were born under whatever remarkable sign had us alive at such an hour. I am proud to be an American. Proud to be a man.

But we are permitted to throw confetti for only a moment or two. Meanwhile, back at the ranch, the problems of society scream for the return of our attention and renewed dedication to their solution.

The late Whitney M. Young who headed the National Urban League said: "The beeps that come from our satellites in chill and distant space tell us something vastly more important than the secrets of the ionosphere. They tell us that this tiny globe that we inherit has become so diminished that every man is in fact every man's next-door neighbor."

The cost of a bomber is a brick school in more than thirty cities. It is two electric plants each serving a town of sixty thousand population. It is two fine, fully equipped hospitals. It is some fifty miles of concrete highway. We pay for a single fighter plane with a half-million bushels of wheat. We pay for a single destroyer with new homes that could have housed more than eight thousand people.

The power of *domino* that took us to the moon must now be applied to the torn seams of the social fabric. The hungry must be fed. The homeless housed. The sick healed. The ignorant taught. The cross of iron which lays upon the back of the international community must be lifted. It is blasphemous to dump the human enterprise back upon the doorstep of Providence.

This is the eloquence of Apollo. The power that pulled that off can and must decontaminate this society of racism, purge its politics of violence, restore cleanliness and decency to its cities, make us brothers and neighbors again. It is a matter of will.

The moon victory says that the present dislocations in human society are correctable—every one of them. Man is a tiger. He is indefatigable. He is invincible. But his heart is vincible. His will is defective. He often loves the wrong things in the right way, and right things in the wrong way. He needs God. He needs forgiveness. He needs love. Until he sets his sights upon life as holy fellowship, until he learns to love the dream of a more just society of men as much as he has learned to love the wonder of space, he will go on in the old ways of death and pessimism concerning himself.

The moon is saying: It's possible! It's possible!

"He who has faith in me will do what I am doing; and he will do greater things still because I am going to the Father" (John 14:12 NEB).

We are not bound to earth any longer. Nor are we bound to a world half-hungry, an America deformed by bigotry, or a church frightened by the "death of God."

A man held, encased in his cupped hands behind his back, a tiny bird. Confidently he challenged another man to guess whether the bird was alive or dead. If he guessed "dead," the man holding the bird would open his hand and let the bird fly away, proving the guesser wrong. If he guessed "alive," the man with the bird would secretly crush him behind his back, then open his hand and expose a lifeless wad of feathers. Either way he was bound to win. One day when he put the question, expecting to have his usual fun and win again, the man who was asked replied: "As you will."

There is no room for helpless determinism in contemporary theology. It is "as we will." This is not to reduce God in size. It is to exalt the love of God, to interpret Him as the Lord of freedom—the God who risked His universe into our hands.

The ride to the moon was not "foreordained." It was a dividend which resulted from an investment of freedom. I hope God is proud. He should be. But His heart will really sing if, from this achievement, we move on to bind up the wounds of this "small and blue and beautiful" earth, and out of the fragments of selfishness, put together a pattern of familyhood—something that will really fly.

Let us never sin again by saying war is inevitable or that racial animosity is imbedded in our blood.

If we can reach the moon, an attitude of defeat about our own redeemability has got to be a lie.

V
A PIECE OF THE ACTION

17
The Truth Is Something You Do

When the song of the angels is stilled,
When the star in the sky is gone,
When the kings and princes are home,
When the shepherds are back with their flocks,
The work of Christmas begins:
    To find the lost,
    To feed the hungry,
    To release the prisoner,
    To bring peace among brothers,
    To make music in the heart.
—HOWARD THURMAN

According to Frederick Speakman, *Love Is Something You Do.* Love is something we are called upon to practice whether we feel like it or not.

The truth is also something we do. Something we discover through participation. Like praying or flying an airplane. Something we experience, rather than memorize.

Jesus continually implored men to do the will of God. "Not every one who says to me, 'Lord, Lord,' shall enter the kingdom of heaven, but he who does the will of my Father..." (Matthew 7:21 RSV).

The truth is more like a foaming, boulder-bouncing river, crashing through canyons of time than it is like a pond or a mute mountain.

Let's imagine a conversation. A man says to Jesus, "I believe You are the Son of God. I believe in Your virgin birth. I believe in the Trinity, the Ascension, the Atonement, the Sacraments. I believe in the miracles, personal salvation, life after death. I believe every word of the Bible is true."

Would Jesus answer, "Good! It is clear you are My disciple"? Or would He say, "You have told Me what you *think*. Have you loved those around you? Have you helped the sick, the poor, the disheartened, the left-out, the ugly, the tired, the lonely?"

There are those who would feel that the truth is closer to the mind than to the hand. That the truth is something one believes in the same way that he believes with his brain that the earth is round, that there is a city called San Francisco, or that, if you mix blue and yellow together, you get green.

But truth is not static. And the Christian faith is not a set of philosophical ideas to which one says yes or no. It is life thrown into a struggle. It is the total involvement of self. Not just mind. It involves the risk of every human security. It is faith expressed through action.

Side by side on the church page were two news stories. One was about a church that was having a problem deciding whether persons could officially represent the congregation at ecclesiastical functions if they had not undergone immersion baptism.

The other told about a church member who had led a movement in the black community to pressure food markets to guarantee quality and prices in the ghetto equal to those on the outside, and not to let these shops become a dumping ground for rotten vegetables and inferior merchandise.

This juxtaposition of concern illustrates the controversy that is pulling the church apart, forcing it to choose.

Is the truth something we cerebrate—or celebrate?

Young people are often told, "When you're in love, you'll *know* it." That may be trite. But it makes the point. Love is more than logic. It sweeps us down truth's river on wild currents. We cannot help ourselves. We do not want to help ourselves. We're in love! We are discovering something so memorable about life, it's as if we were the first person in the world ever to have felt such things.

We have similar sensations and insights when, for the first

time, we get involved in political action or in doing something to change the world.

We cannot tolerate a dividing line between belief and action. Some evangelism rests on the assumption that it is the goal of faith to extract "confessions of faith." If a person says, "I believe in Jesus Christ," then, according to this particular strategy, the *main* function of the church will have been fulfilled. A man has believed. He has been converted. He has been asked a question; he has given the right answer.

This may be the first step a man takes on his journey to God. But it runs the danger of becoming a placebo. A "decision" can lead down a road of "cheap grace" if it is imagined that saying "Lord, Lord" equals obedience. Jesus, "Your mother and your brothers are outside, asking for you." He answers, "Whoever does the will of God is my brother, and sister, and mother" (Mark 3:33, 35 RSV).

The truth is not simply something we read in a book; it is something we experience in our encounters with each other and with a world in trouble.

Some of us don't want to be changed. We like ourselves the way we are. We don't want to be upset. We don't want to be challenged. We don't like people who talk loudly or don't take a bath every day. We don't like those who create turmoil with marches or ask for a new deal in a strange accent. It is a temptation for the secure to settle for a faith which reassures rather than threatens. But the truth is something we do.

There were two boys. The father asked them to go and work in his field. One said, "I go, sir," but did not. The other said, "No," but went.

Doers do not need to trumpet their convictions. They show. They shine. Our presence at worship proves nothing—except that we care.

Salvation is not a matter of being doctrinally inspected and stamped "approved." It is falling into the river, trying to swim, feeling the buoyancy of the water. It's not so much being checked out for heaven as it is being fitted for life in a dangerous world.

The late James Pike wrote a book and asked his friend Paul

Tillich to suggest a title. Tillich's choice: *Doing the Truth.* Another James put it still better. He said a man who hears the call of God and does nothing about it is like the man who glances at himself in a mirror, and then goes upon his way forgetting what he saw. But a man who *does,* who acts the best he can, even though his mind is tangled with doubt, is bound to discover that, clumsy and imperfectly performed as his discipleship is, freedom has filled his cup—even run over and puddled into a stream which, whether he knows it or not, is bringing greenness to a discouraged mankind.

18
Jonah Was a Cop-out

Jonah: Please, please, what do you want from my life? He won't leave me alone. All these years I've been running—a traveler—Jonah, the traveler, representing Top Hat; Braces For the Trousers; Fair Lady Fancy Buttons; Hold Tight Hair Grips —only good brands in the suitcase. Ask them in Tarshish, ask them in Aleppo, in Carthage even; they all know Jonah ben Amittai, regular call once a month for more than thirty years. I don't complain, only I'm tired of running, that's all. Now at last I'm tired. I get this good pitch here— at last—so I shouldn't have to run with a suitcase any more. And still he nags me. All right. I heard. I'm going. What happens to me shouldn't happen to a dog.

Angel: [Later in the play] We are the dogs of God.

—WOLF MANKOWITZ

One night when I, then a high-school student, was walking along Walnut Street, I encountered the minister of our church. He was on his way home from a meeting.

We stopped and chatted for a few minutes in the shadow of the post office. He said he had been with a group that had spent the evening discussing Jonah. It was late and we did not talk long, but I remember thinking, as I left him, Jonah? The story of the man who survived three days in the belly of a whale? How could a bunch of adults spend a *whole* evening talking about that?

Since then, I have found out a few more things about Jonah.

Jonah is a fish story with a hook, a fish story which isn't fishy at all.

To understand Jonah we first have to get historically oriented. Most Old Testament writings pivot around two events. One is the escape at the Red Sea from Pharaoh and forty hard years in the desert. The other is the destruction of the Temple in 586 B.C. and the dragging off of God's people into exile. We cannot understand the Old Testament apart from these two happenings.

In reading the King James Version of Psalm 137, for example, how much more meaningful its words are if we read them in the context of the exile experience rather than in a devotional vacuum:

> By the rivers of Babylon,
> There we sat down, yea, we wept,
> When we remembered Zion.
> We hanged our harps
> Upon the willows in the midst thereof.
> For there they that carried us away captive required of us a song;
> And they that wasted us required of us mirth,
> Saying, Sing us one of the songs of Zion.
> How shall we sing the Lord's song
> In a strange land?

(Meaning: Dance for us, you stupid slaves. We want to see how funny you look!)

Where Jonah enters the picture is at the close of this seventy-year period of being refugees.

Under the administration of the Persian conqueror Darius the Jews are allowed to return home and rebuild the old theocracy. A few go back, determined to rebuild the Temple and reinstitute the former religious customs. But the Jewishness of most has been diluted. Younger people have grown less interested in being distinctive. Many have intermarried with the Babylonians. Those who do return are the pious, those determined to keep their identity intact.

Ezra and Nehemiah are the books which tell what happens during this period. At this time the Psalms are collected and made up into a hymnbook for congregational worship.

In the midst of all this, smugness develops. Great stress is placed on the strict observance of Jewish law—the rituals, the food laws, the prohibition against marriage to foreigners.

Against this sort of elitism the author of Jonah strikes. He does it with a barbed tale which pokes sophisticated shame at a people so caught up in the formalities of theology they have forgotten how to spell grace.

It does not cheapen the Bible to confess that it contains a cartoon. The Bible is a library with many interesting departments. It contains history, music, law codes, poetry, plays, letters, folklore, biography, and a comic page.

Cartoons slash and teach better than words. I like one which shows a middle-aged man sitting dejectedly, glass in hand at a bar. "Okay, so you're forty—you've lived half your life. But look on the bright side. If you were a horse, you'd already have been dead fifteen years."

What the author of Jonah, through his caricature, protests is the attitude of a people who are making a big deal out of what it means to be Jewish. They claim they have a message and a righteousness from God that is for all men, and that they are "a light to the Gentiles." But down deep they care little about their neighbors. What they are mostly interested in is maintaining their own turf—keeping separate and superior to the pagans who live around them.

Jonah is really Israel. He is a man who tries to run away from God's call to be an agent of love. He is asked by God to go preach the good news of God to Nineveh. He resists. He hides aboard a ship headed in the opposite direction. This is the first point of the story—the temptation all men face to run away from God and responsibility.

Then, a supernatural occurrence follows. There is a storm. Jonah is thrown into the sea but then is rescued by the intervention of Providence. This wakes him up. Awake to the realization that he can't outpoint God, he goes, with pouting and reluctance, and does what God asked him to do in the first place. He preaches. The Ninevites repent. Rather than being pleased, though, at their response, he is irritated. "See!" he mutters, "I knew that's what would happen! Now these people have part of the action, too. We can't enjoy our privileged status any more." His mouth twists as if he had just bitten into a stick of quinine. This is the second point of the story. There is a difference about honestly caring about the people around you, and pretending that you do. Jonah preached the love of God to Nineveh, but his heart was not in it. When they responded, he acted like a brat.

The final panel has the prophet out near the edge of the city, dealing with another problem. He's still angry with God, but his attention is diverted by a hot sun overhead. The temperature is very high. At first it appears that Jonah is lucky. He has found a small shade tree to protect himself against the brutal heat. But God sends a worm to kill the tree. It wilts, and the shade disappears.

Jonah gives up. He says, "All right, Lord, You win. Take my life. I've had it! I'm through!"

Then God speaks, gently, to His troubled servant.

"Jonah, is it right for you to be upset like this? You're mad about the tree. And angry with Me. If you can worry about a little thing like the tree, don't you think I have a right to worry about a whole city like Nineveh?"

Jonah is a story about a man who tried to run away from God.

Jonah is a story about a man whose compassion had a quality of phoniness about it.

Jonah is a story about a man who was so wrapped up in his own situation he couldn't see the larger world and its needs.

The real prophet in this book is not Jonah. The prophet is the writer, the storyteller, the Bill Mauldin who, through a story that is a mixture of comedy and Christ, has left both Jews and Christians with something to think about forever.

Much of religion is escape. It cannot honestly confront the world, so it drops the subject and says: The world isn't important; let's talk about the world on the other side of death. Poverty, ignorance, and social hopelessness are providential forces over which man has no control. Forget about them; dream about a "Beautiful Isle of Somewhere."

And we become escape-minded in our personal lives. Sex and drug experimentation, astrology, peak psychology, travel, positive thinking. We try everything. We hide behind hedges, security guards, and dark glasses. We try to get away from the anger of the times—shut our ears, shut our eyes. Tell the church to get lost. Tell our neighbors to get lost. Tell. Tell the times to get lost. Run. Run. Give me another drink.

But there comes a moment when we lie breathlessly on the ground and say, "All right, God, I can't run anymore. What do You want?"

God replies, "The first thing I want is for you to stop running. Is that too much to ask? What are you running from? Don't you know you belong to Me, that I have created you not for anxiety and fear, but for trust, service, and joy?"

As Christians we confess we are brothers. We bet our lives upon a Man who said to us, in what will go down as the most poignant comment He ever made: "As you did it to one of the least of these my brethren, you did it to me." We endorse the words of the Great Commission: "Go into all the world and preach the gospel." But we are slow to reach out in compassionate involvement to these "least ones," and we "wouldn't want our daughter to marry one." We are more worked up about our taxes than the fact that some people may die before we can reach them. It is a now familiar charge by young people that, when they do certain things we have spent much of their lives trying to persuade them to do, we take umbrage and accuse them of uncooperative behavior. We pray for peace and say we are for it. But if peace brings deep economic reductions in our standard of living, we begin to resemble Jonah who became disgusted when Someone took him seriously, gave him what he said he wanted.

A minister made an appeal for his people to respond to the call to go to distant places in the world to live among the poverty-stricken and to institute programs to help them. When his own daughter responded, he wasn't sure he wanted her to go. Jonah asks: How honest are we in wanting our ideals to be converted into reality?

And Jonah is upset over what happens to his dear little shade tree. Frequently, we get ourselves worked up over some little thing that goes wrong in the day's routine. The car has a flat tire. A window won't open. Somebody got a spot on the rug. The dog got loose. The plumber charged too much. A shoestring broke. One of the children told us a lie and our whole edifice of self-confidence fell in like a house of cards. Someone passed us by without speaking. The toast was too brown. We got a cold. A traffic ticket. In such moments we decided life is hardly worth it. We find ourselves depressed by little things that do not deserve that kind of importance.

While our toast is burning up, other families are mourning the deaths of sons in Viet Nam or dealing with fast-moving cancer. Some people are out of jobs and looking for work. Others live with incurable mental illness. Others face life inside a prison. Still others, unable to kick a habit, contemplate suicide. The Population Reference Bureau says 324,000 new babies enter the world on an average day. About ten thousand older persons die that same day, either of starvation or malnutrition.

Jonah is an appeal to look beyond ourselves. It is the call to forsake the little for the large, to replace things with persons as that which most deeply concerns us. People who get upset over trivia are letting out a hasty secret about themselves—which is that, at the center of their world, there's a gilt-edged *I*.

When Jesus was asked to validate His ministry by performing miracles, He declined—saying the only sign men could count upon would be the Sign of Jonah. Many words have been written in an attempt to explain what He meant by that.

I'm not sure what the answer is. It must have something to do with the authority of truth itself. Jonah went to Nineveh with an invitation to welcome God into the life of that city. This was all the "sign" he had—no tricks, no letters of credit, no purple badge stamped "official."

He comes eternally to men without any grand portfolio—only with gracious words upon His lips and hope in His eyes and a set of promises we can accept or reject.

To say yes is to set out toward a city. Is to buy into a dream. Is to have the courage to hear what the funny little story of Jonah is actually saying to you.

19
If You Were Arrested for Being a Christian, How Much Evidence Would There Be Against You?

This seems a cheerful world, Donatus, when I view it from this garden under the shadow of these vines. But if I climbed some great mountain and looked over the wide lands, you know very well what I would see. Brigands on the high roads, pirates on the seas . . . under all roofs misery and selfishness. It is really a bad world, Donatus, an incredibly bad world. Yet in the midst of it I have found a quiet and holy people. They arise before dawn to sing hymns to their savior God. They have discovered a joy which is a thousand times better than any pleasure. They are despised and persecuted, but they have overcome the world. These people, Donatus, are the Christians and I am one of them.

—CYPRIAN

Charles was returning to Los Angeles from Oklahoma City on a plane. An hour before it was due to land, a passenger became confused and wanted off. He was a large, heavy-set man. At first, the stewardess was able to keep him in his seat, but he was soon up again, speaking loudly and causing panic. Charles offered to move and take the seat next to the troubled traveler. The man's original seatmate readily agreed. By the time the flight reached Los Angeles International Airport, the agitated man was composed again. Charles followed him off the plane and stayed at his side until he made connections with family members who were there waiting to meet him.

Officials on the ground had been alerted about trouble in the air, and a representative of the airline was there at the gate as the people deplaned. Noticing how Charles handled the upset passenger with gentleness and understanding, the airline agent asked, "Are you trained in working with people like this?"

"No," said Charles, "I was just trying to be a friend."

This is the other half of Kitty Genovese.

Are Christians recognizable in the crowd? Or have they dissolved into the pagan push and lost, even among themselves, the feeling of Saltness?

It is not the goal of a Christian to be conspicuous. He is warned against making a noise about his faith or wearing empathy embroidered on his sleeves. But the Man who gave that warning, also said: "A city set on a hill cannot be hid. . . . Let your light so shine before men" (Matthew 5:14, 16 RSV).

The letter in the headnote was written by Cyprian seventeen hundred years ago. It prompted my own paraphrase:

> This seems like a cheerful world, dear listener, when I view it from the gracious environs of Claremont, with its proud lawns and gentle trees, its well-educated citizens, and lovely churches. But if I were to climb up to the top of Mt. Baldy and look out over the wider panorama of Southern California, you know very well what I would see; frustration and despair, vast quantities of human emptiness. I would see half of all Mexican-American youngsters dropping out of school by the time they reached the eighth grade. I would see in Los Angeles the pornographic capital of the world, uncountable families torn asunder by debts and drugs and the failure of communication. In many ways it is a bad, broken world, dear listener, but within it the spirit of renewal and reconciliation is still alive. It is a particular concern of the people who call themselves Christians, and I am one of them.

If you were arrested for being a Christian, how much evidence would there be against you? What is there in your life or about your behavior that would link you with the crime of loving God?

In Nathaniel Hawthorne's *Scarlet Letter,* Hester Prynne, accused of adultery, wore a crimson *A*. In Nazi Germany, Jews were forced to display the star of David. Sometimes Christians wear the cross or a miniature fish. But the "stamp of Jesus" is more than a medal. For Saint Paul it was more closely identified with the look in a man's eyes or the welts on his back.

What kind of a case does the world have against you? With what would you be charged that would link you with the Christ conspiracy?

In *Leonard versus the State of Ohio,* an appellate court furnished this definition: "Evidence is that which demonstrates, makes clear, or ascertains the truth of the fact or point in issue, either on one side or the other." Most of us know about circumstantial evidence, state's evidence, hearsay evidence. We know what character witnesses are, what expert witnesses are. After a dozen years of watching "Dragnet" and "Mission Impossible," we qualify as fair judges of admissable evidence.

For the purposes of this chapter the Fifth Amendment is suspended. Bear in mind that, rather than trying to exonerate ourselves, we are trying to find out if there is enough evidence to book us, to support a finding of guilty of the charge of plotting to conquer the world using as our *modus operandi* the strategies of faith, hope, and love.

First, there is the evidence of places where we've been seen. Would a stakeout reveal we had been observed receiving baptism as a sign of membership in the movement? Or that we were spotted eating and drinking a ceremonial meal called The Lord's Supper? Would the prosecutor be able to say to the jury that wiretaps had picked up the sound of our voices saying a suppertime grace, or meeting with other defendants to study subversive writings known as the New Testament? Would the D.A. be able to prove we had been tracked into the neighborhoods of the poor, into the homes of people in trouble, or that we had identified ourselves with them in organized efforts to lift the burden of being black or rising above the handicap of not knowing how to speak English?

But we're just getting started! Bring on exhibits A, B, C, and D. Find a table. Spread out before the jury the truly incriminating pieces.

Some evidence is known as *prima facie* evidence. Simply by looking at it, it appears to accuse; it states arguments of its own. In law it is called *res ipsa loquitur:* the thing that speaks for itself. A child struck by a car in a school-zone crosswalk means a clear case of negligence. It is evidence which, until it is refuted, by the nature of the accident, imputes culpability to the driver. What is there in our lives that shouts, You are one of *them?*

Does our checkbook state a clear case of involvement with

the ministry of Jesus? Our correspondence? Do we mention faith in the people we write to? Each time Thomas Merton signed his name to a letter, he made, to the left of his signature, a tiny cross. Perhaps that's not your brand of bearing witness, but it is better than silence. Are there books on the faith in your library? Is there an altar in your home, some mark of identity on your walls?

One night, after an hour of discussing politics, Chiang Kai-shek said to a guest that he and Mrs. Chiang wanted him to stay to join in family prayers. Later, this was reported:

> The General took the Bible in his hands and began to read a passage. Then we all joined in prayer led by the General himself. He began with a simple expression of gratitude for the courage of the nation under fire. He then prayed for strength and energy for the men in the fields of labor and for those who were on the firing line. He prayed that God would give him strength and, in a special way, wisdom and direction that he might not abandon his people.
>
> He prayed for the Japanese Christians . . . and placed himself in God's hands, praying that he might know the divine will. Then after an half hour . . . the Generalissimo and his wife rose from their knees, shook hands with their friend, and bade him good night.

"You are accused. . . ."

The voice echoes across the too warm air of the courtroom, as the judge swivels right to left, then back again.

"You are accused of certain forms of behavior which do not accord with commonly accepted standards. To wit: You have been known to forgive persons who have offended you and treated you unfairly. You have accepted persons different from yourself as brothers; you have not merely tolerated or respected them, conceded them rights equal to those you claimed for yourself; you have embraced them, treated them like you would members of your own family in contradiction of the tradition which says that 'they like to be with their own kind.'

"You are further charged with taking upon your shoulders the problems of other people—especially the weak and the poor—and treating them as seriously as you would needs of your own. In one instance you went into debt for medical expenses for a child you scarcely knew. You opened your home to a foster child who had special problems with health."

The case is building and the jurors look as if they have heard enough to make up their minds.

The prosecutor is on his feet, interlocking his fingers, looking at the floor, striding up and down in front of the box. He still has a final point to make before he rests his case.

"This man," he begins—and a little nervous shiver goes up and down your spine because you know he's talking about you—"this man even walks like a Christian. He doesn't even need to say a word. Whether he is walking to his car, riding the elevator up to the sixteenth floor, or mowing his lawn, he gives you the impression that he interprets life as a flow of gift—as something he didn't deserve. He has an infectious sparkle to his life. This man is guilty of Christianity in the first degree!"

Camus has a phrase: "The grouping of men we need is a grouping of men resolved to speak out clearly and to pay up personally."

If we are guilty as charged we can expect some discomfort, some embarrassment, some opposition, some rejection, some pain. Unless we are ready to pay the price we will have to be acquitted and turned loose.

A medical missionary to Labrador, Dr. Wilfred Grenfell, once said of Jesse Halsey, a pastor whose life made a sharp imprint upon my own: "I have seen more of Jesus Christ in you than anyone I have ever known."

I knew Grenfell had said that, and I looked at Jess with the Grenfell statement in mind. I found why he had said it. Halsey was guilty, guilty of ferreting out little people who were having a hard time and filling their pockets with unexpected love, guilty of modesty, guilty of caring more about what was in people's hearts than in their heads, guilty of walking thoughtfully at sunset along the beach or puttering with the startling possibilities of stained glass chips.

Thomas said of Jesus: "Unless I see in his hands the print of the nails, and place my finger in the mark of the nails, ... I will not believe" (John 20:25 RSV). He found them!

If we are lovers of God and servants of Christ, the CIA will find a dossier on us four inches thick. We can't keep our connection with Christ a secret, and if we ever get arrested on the charge of being His friend, we'll go to jail for a thousand years.

Unless we happen to know the Warden. In that case He just might wink at us, slip us a spare key, and look the other way.

20
How Do You Feel When People Ask You What You Do for a Living?

Work is love made visible.

—KAHLIL GIBRAN

Meet a lucky guy—me. I love my job. I wouldn't know how to separate what I do for pleasure from the things I do for pay. I am a minister. When people ask me what I do for a living, I grin and say, "I'm in The Service."

I wrote this letter to my son to try to explain my "luck":

Dear Jim,

I have tried to make it clear, ever since you were old enough to understand and talk about such things, that I have no desire to turn you into a minister of religion. I think you believe me, though we sometimes joke about it. Unless the ministry is something you want more than any other thing, it will be as dull as dishwater.

My prayer is that you will wind up being as enthusiastic about your niche in life as Vince Lombardi was about coaching football, as Mike Nichols is about producing theatre, or as Alan Shephard is about space flight.

These are people who have been "grabbed" by something. I enjoy the ministry because I feel like I've been "grabbed" by one of the biggest things going: dealing with what it means to be human, and faithful to the God who gives us life.

My "work" as an ordained minister began the first Sunday of June, 1949. I gave a sermon in the First Presbyterian Church of Indianola, Iowa, called "Peter's Shadow."

I doubt if you remember the story. In the first days of the church, following the death of Jesus, Peter, James, and John were moving around together, trying to carry on the things they had seen their Leader do. Their efforts met with striking success, and the people concluded that these men were in possession of miraculous powers.

> More than ever believers were added to the Lord . . . so that they even carried out the sick into the streets, and laid them on beds and pallets, that as Peter came by at least his shadow might fall on some of them. [Acts 5:14, 15 RSV]

"We all cast a shadow," I said that day. We affect the people we are with every time we are with them. We wind up making others more hopeful about themselves, or less.

The congregation has probably forgotten that day by now, but, when your mother and I said goodbye at the church door five years later, with tight throats and trembling speech, we knew shadows had overlapped.

We do not hear much today about the call to preach. Churches still "call" ministers, and some of the old language is still current, but now we think and speak more about men who choose the ministry, than a ministry that chooses men.

I admit feeling drawn into the ministry then by an irresistible force. I still do.

There were no ministers in the family before me. My mother had the most to do with exposing me to the strange magnetism of the Scriptures, and she gave me some lasting lessons on personal accountability. Taught me love by loving me. In my boyhood church in Atlantic, Iowa, I also had experiences which deepened my feelings of self-acceptance and wonder. Having no brothers or sisters, or television, I went often to the library for something to do. An element of loneliness became part of me then. I usually arose at 4:30 A.M. to deliver newspapers. The quietness of a small town at 4:30, with no other companion except a dog, is a good setting to pose questions to yourself.

I remember good times you and I have had together since then—helping get the *Louisville Courier-Journal* delivered during hard rains and heavy snows. I remember a couple of mornings you overslept.

Add three summers at senior-high conference, four years at Simpson College with lots of personal contact with my teachers, four years at sea, and three years in law school, and the result was someone interested in finding out all he could about those meanings which lie at the center of history and life.

I want you to know why I like the ministry. I'll be fair and give the other side, too.

The ministry provides a chance to keep growing mentally as long as you live. A minister has to read continuously and update his knowledge. He is not expected to know the answers, but he must know the questions. He must read the Bible, periodicals, novels, plays, history, and biography. He must be familiar with Bonhoeffer and Bultmann, Bradbury and Barth.

He should count on seeing the new films. This is often what

people are discussing. They will probably be pinpointing pain.

He must develop a capacity to listen. He must recognize that young people get hung up on drugs, not because of drugs, but because of noneloquent feelings about themselves. He must recognize that marriages fail because of conflicts in ideas about personal worth or because of the failures of honesty or communication.

He must go to the hospitals, the mortuaries, the nursing homes, the jails, the campuses, the factories where people are busy with their hands. He must be at home in places where people are poor, desperate, and hostile. Visit, if he can, the music center and parks where older people sit alone, their minds forty years away.

He should come to know people in city government, the schools, the YMCA and YWCA.

When he takes time to enjoy his family, he shouldn't feel guilty. That is part of human completeness. I could write for hours on the help I have received from your mother and you four children. That must be another letter, another time.

I hope you're thinking, That doesn't sound as bad as I thought. It might even be fun.

Everything we *want* to do is fun. Football practice leaves you bone tired. Replacing a carburetor can mean two hours bending over the hood of a car, but it can also be the greatest fun in the world.

The ministry is fun if you mingle with people, grapple with ideas, become involved in shaping your times. Every engagement with another human being is a chance to express and to enlarge your humanity. You are always being reminded how exciting children can be, how keen a seventeen-year-old boy can be, how wonderful older people can be, how much joy there is in the world, how much need.

Still, it's hard to be adequate.

I've never forgotten what Virgil Hancher, former president of the University of Iowa, said to me about ministers. I was in law school at the time, but his sentence stuck. He said,

"Ministers tend not to be very rigorous thinkers." That was a useful warning.

Ministers, as you know, are often portrayed by Hollywood as doddering and stupid. They putter and puff and repeat their little sugar rubrics, oblivious of real life. That's not the ministry, and I hope it's not me.

Ministers also have a responsibility to put the runaway events of history in perspective. The church often has been twelve paces behind, baptizing a new order after braver men have suffered it into existence and acceptance. But that is changing.

I sometimes think wistfully about my weekly exhortations to brotherhood from the pulpit in the early 1950s—words which left things about where they were, while a handful of college kids in a North Carolina lunch counter were setting in motion a movement that will eventually cleanse this land of a vicious disease.

The Bible is about hunger, murder, love, fear, anger, debts, adultery, wealth, poverty, demon possession, and the Josephs who became princes. Ministers must turn the gospel loose in the world. It must enter Wall Street, Congress, the Sunset Strip, every battlefield of man—or become introverted and false. Jesus was world-centered, not church-centered. So must we be. Christians major in life, not religion.

Life is changing. I read somewhere that the idea of surfing is to ride the turbulence without succumbing to it, that you can't have fun surfing on a slow wave, and you can't surf at all on a frozen one. I should take some surfing lessons to learn how to keep my balance. Change is the cost of new experiences. Without it, creation would stop, heaven disappear. Changes which tear at the church hardest now involve a switch from lovely buildings and spellbinding addresses to more attention to the wounds of the world, to advocacy of the cause of those too weak to speak for themselves.

A minister is a question-asker.

He asks a question, then repeats it. He's charged with seeing that key questions are not lost in the scuffle toward success: Who is man? What is freedom? To whom does man owe his creation? Who is my neighbor? How shall I deal with the person who wrongs me? What does it mean to die? Who is God? Where is peace? What or who deserves the ultimate allegiance of my life?

He is also a man called Help.

Usually he cannot provide a solution. But he can make known the interest God has in the problem. He can help people see the difference between being honest with themselves, or deceitful. He can point them toward the Light. He can stand beside a grave, kneel beside a bed, or say to one with an anxious face, "Let's go get a cup of coffee." He can be a little human head of land on which to beach a boat when the storm is at its height.

He can be the means through which other people discover their own ministries. If he tries to be the church himself, a star performer with an audience, he will fall flat on his face. If he can inspire others to hunger and thirst for righteousness, lay their lives upon the line, then the famous Galilean will be seen walking again upon our streets of the town and the resurrection will be confirmed.

The things that make the ministry hardest are not the hours, not the free advice, not the embarrassment of being treated as if you were a third sex, nor of being apologized to for a dirty story told in your presence. It is continuing to take the message of Jesus seriously, keeping yourself from letting Christianity become a game of words rather than a gamble for your life.

It's not in trying to love your opposition. If you cannot do that, you'd better try out for a different sport. It is in trying to balance the function of prophet and pastor, mixing correction and comfort, plumb line and myrrh in the right proportion. It is in having to be radically dissatisfied with yourself. It is the feeling of being pulled apart as Jesus was in Jerusalem when they stretched his arms and legs upon that board and fastened them there with spikes.

Living daily in and through the lives of others is thrilling and mellowing. It gives you a sense of fantastic privilege. It helps you look at your own days and difficulties against a broad backdrop of trouble, helps you feel gratitude and even strangely peaceful about your own death.

These are confused and anxious times for the church. But why should the church be spared? They are restive moments for everyone—leaders in government, leaders in higher education, blacks trying to choose between an old dead order and reckless militancy, and not finding very much in between. Youth trying to hammer out new designs of commitment in the secular city.

Life remains a laboratory of wonder as long as men remember God and have the courage to set the events of a few years in the context of the All.

If there is anxiety, there is hope; if there is frustration, there is a determination. I am glad to be one who keeps pulling on the bell ropes that say: Keep on!

Love,
Your Dad

VI
IS NECESSARY FOR PEACE

21
Make Peace With Yesterday

I'm glad that God takes every worn-out day and burns it up in sunset;
All mistakes, the little triumphs, and the futile cares
Are gathered into one bonfire that breaks in flame against the banks of sky.

I think He likes to see it burn and stand beside it till the last grey ashes fall.
And then across the fretful thoroughfares, over the troubled roofs and petty wars
Out of lonely heights of the unknown a clean wind blows all tangled up with stars.

—ANONYMOUS

"Forgetting what lies behind and straining forward to what lies ahead, I press on. . . ." (Philippians 3:13 RSV).

Those words have been recited a million times since Paul wrote to a miniscule congregation in Philippi. They are full of music. They make a great text for a New Year's sermon. They also contain a problem: forgetting.

Forgetting the past is not only difficult, bordering on the impossible, it is, by another way of looking at it, what God asks us *not* to do.

Some things deserve to be forgotten, and this is, most likely, what Paul is thinking about. But some things deserve to be remembered forever.

The process of working out these differences within ourselves is helpfully summed up by Rabbi Robert Kahn of Houston, Texas: "Make your peace with yesterday."

We can't change the past, but we have a lot to say about the attitude we take toward it.

Some events of our lives we cherish and like to relive in memory; other things we would like to forget. Making peace with yesterday embraces both.

The past has power both to bless and blight, to help and hurt.

A criticism made of the church by college students is that the church is too much dominated by the past. It is forever discussing what happened two thousand years ago. Instead of dealing enthusiastically with the present, or optimistically with the future, it threshes the same old tired straw. Rehearses the same old stories. It is mired in an age which has disappeared, along with the three-storied universe and three-month crossings of the great oceans.

There is a validity to such criticisms, for God is not static and neither is faith. God is living, contemporary. He wants us to take our times as seriously as Biblical people took theirs.

We can affirm this, and still admit that it is important to find direction for the present by understanding the past.

We ought to make no apology for the church as the Remembering Community. We are the People of God, the Fellowship of the Forgiven, the Company of the Committed. But we are also Professional Rememberers. We are called to remember that God is the Source of life and of meaning. To remember that Bethlehem marks an intersection of eternity and time. And to remember who we are. In us the past is gathered up and stated. Many of us stand on the shoulders of parents who did not have a college education but who saw to it that we did. We do not struggle with 84,000 problems because others struggled with them and handed on their results.

In 1954, I agonized over long months with several families whose children were dying or threatened with extreme handicaps as a result of polio. Today that illness has been conquered. The March of Dimes has turned its attention to birth defects and other medical problems. Like Goliath, cancer, too, will one day fall, and man will look up and give thanks.

To remember the past is the first step toward becoming human. G. A. Studdert-Kennedy said God gave us memories in order that we might have "June roses in December." But it is more than a case of having memories. The past is part of us. It is woven into our blood, our values, and dreams. In us the past continues its life. "Love never ends" (1 Corinthians 13:8 RSV).

Youth should not be asked to stand watch over old values. But there is no way to dispense with the need for a creative attitude toward the past. The Christian faith is not nostalgia. It calls men to remember so that they can *be*.

The bad side of the past—the crippling side—involves items of experience which deserve to be cut away and cast upon the wind. Wrote Rabbi Kahn:

> Don't let yesterday destroy today. You have had failures in the past. You have failed in business, failed a course, failed a friend, failed your family. But who has not? No one is perfect, no one is all successful. Don't dwell on those failures. Make peace with yesterday.

God's Word, with respect to the things we regret is simply: "Let go. Let go. Let it go. Make peace with yesterday. I forgive you. Be free. Accept a new beginning."

But it's not that simple.

Paul Wellman's *The Chain* is about a young Episcopal priest. Though this minister is effective in his work, he is held back in his life, and in his loves, by a mysterious secret which isn't revealed until the final page. In those final paragraphs he is brought, broken and bleeding, into an operating room, following an accident, where his awful burden is discovered. As a youth he had one day, in a fit of angry temper, struck his brother and accidentally killed him. To atone for this wrong, and as lifelong penance, he had had a chain welded about his body.

It sounds bizarre, and is. But life carries us into desperate regions. We enter strange territories of the heart. We reach levels of suffering we didn't know existed. What sounds to us as extreme one day, may not the next.

Make peace with yesterday.

Sometimes, it's not a mistake. Simply a terrible yearning to reconstruct the past, to go over and over it a certain set of hours again—thinking how things might have turned out differently. The steeplechase of the imagination which never ends.

We can't change the past, but we can't stop wanting to change it either. That battle has produced many soldiers. It is a hard one to win, but we are assured by the fellowship of saints that some victories are possible.

Make peace with yesterday?

Rabbi Kahn is wrong. We can't "make" peace ourselves. We can only hold out our hands and receive peace from the God of Comfort.

We can help to deal with yesterday in a constructive manner by forgiving others, qualifying for our own forgiveness. The most important word in the Lord's Prayer is *as*. We are forgiven to the same extent that *we* forgive.

We must take some responsibility for our lives, but not all. To assume that we are exclusively responsible for our lives is to say that God created the world, then went on vacation.

I keep going back to this comeuppance by Harvard professor Henry A. Murray in his article "The Meaning and Content of Individuality in Contemporary America":

> [Man] is not able to decide that the heart shall keep on beating. He is not able to decide that a plentiful supply of energy and enthusiasm will be available next morning. He is not able to decide to fall in love. He is not able to decide that fresh and significant ideas shall spring to mind to enliven his conversation or to advance his thought. He cannot choose to choose what he will choose. From first to last he is utterly dependent for his being, for the capacity to

sense, feel, think, and act, for the delight of living, upon the perfect orchestration of billions of uncontrollable, irreversible, and inscrutable goings on within him. And yet his objective knowledge of these facts does not bring him round to wisdom. He takes it all for granted; accepts it without reverence, without gratitude and without grace. The fault, as I see it, lies in a kind of hydrocephalus of the ego. The ego shouts "I am the master of my fate!" and a minute later one tiny embolus slits the thinspun life and puts an end to all that nonsense.

Everyone gets to die. Hidden inside the word *heaven* is a truth with which we are intimately involved. The victory shout of the Christian man is that the good is never lost. Love is imperishable. But man is soul and the future is not a blank. New life, which begins in Christ, carries us beyond the farthermost horizon of knowledge. We do not know where paradise is, but we know why it is.

We also help make peace with yesterday when we flood our minds with thoughts about life's new possibilities—thoughts of countries still waiting to be discovered, tasks waiting to be completed.

Here are my "rules": (1) Forgive. (2) Take some responsibility for your life, but not all of it. (3) Remember God has set eternity in your heart and promised that you will share in it. (4) Look ahead.

This means that we must live today in the light of what tomorrow will be, as well as in the light of what yesterday had been.

A college student made this remark: "I'm trying to live my life as if the future had already begun." That's a good place to stand.

Wrote Rollo May in *Love and Will*:

> We stand on the peak of the consciousness of previous ages and their wisdom is available to us. History —that selective treasure house of the past which

each age bequeaths to those that follow—has formed us in the present so that we may embrace the future. What does it matter if our insights, the new forms which play around the fringes of our minds, always lead us into virginal land where, like it or not, we stand on strange and bewildering ground? The only way out is ahead, and our choice is whether we shall cringe from it or affirm it.

"The only way out is ahead." This is what Paul is driving at. It is God's Word of hope to persons who have been spending time in the valley of trouble.

It is God's Word to America and to history. God's novel continues to unfold. And He seeks from each of us some flashes of evidence that we have heard His voice and believed.

22
Peace Is a Journey

In a universe whose size is beyond human imagining, where our world floats like a dust mote in the void of night, men have grown inconceivably lonely. We scan the time scale and the mechanisms of life itself for portents and signs of the invisible. As the only thinking mammals on the planet—perhaps the only thinking animals in the entire sidereal universe—the burden of consciousness has grown heavy upon us. We watch the stars, but the signs are uncertain. We uncover the bones of the past and seek for our origins. There is a path there, but it appears to wander. The vagaries of the road may have a meaning, however; it is thus we torture ourselves.

Lights come and go in the night sky. Men, troubled at last by the things they build, may toss in their sleep and dream bad dreams, or lie awake while the meteors whisper greenly overhead. But nowhere in all space or on a thousand worlds will there be men to share our loneliness. There may be wisdom; there may be power; somewhere across space great instruments, handled by strange, manipulative organs, may stare vainly at our floating cloud wrack, their owners yearning as we yearn. Nevertheless, in the nature of life and in the principles of evolution we have had our answer. Of men elsewhere, and beyond, there will be none forever.
—LOREN EISELEY

One morning after Sunday school, something violent happened in the churchyard. I remember more about the fight than the lesson.

A leading role was played by George Remington. George *was* a leader, but he had a habit of tormenting younger kids who weren't as confident or as quick with their hands as he was.

Sticking up for his own rights came hard for my cousin Frank, and George had a way of picking on him. He would steal his cap, trip him from behind, do anything he could think of to reduce Frank to tears.

On this particular day George was up to his old tricks, and a circle had formed to watch the action. Thoughts of Abraham, or of Paul sailing past Malta, were forgotten in this 11:05 confrontation.

Seeing Frank was about to get the worst of it, I yielded to my indignation, stepped into the middle of the circle and told this bully to leave Frank alone. He turned to me, his eyes blazing. "What are you going to do about it?" he inquired.

He had hardly finished his sentence when I unleashed my

fist and hit him so hard he landed on his rear, his lip spurting blood. Everyone in the circle stood transfixed—looking grave—wondering if there would be another round.

There wasn't. Sunday school was over. So was the fight. As Frank, his younger brother John, and I walked home through the autumn sunlight that morning, I felt a peace flowing through me so satisfying that my skin still tingles thinking about it.

Self-discovery and self-esteem turn on peace—peace with God, peace within ourselves, peace among ourselves. Peace is the largest issue of man. The Jews have a word for it—the most beautiful word in the Hebrew language: *shalom.* What is peace? Are we sure we want it?

Each Sunday, Christians gather to pray for peace. Jesus is the Prince of Peace.

An inverted *Y,* inside a circle, is the peace symbol meaning nuclear disarmament. More than ten years of war in Indochina has made us desperately interested in peace.

But what if peace for us means war for someone else? My altercation with George left me exhilarated. But how did it leave him?

The peace we want, and the peace we are willing to die to gain, has to be peace understood as a process rather than as a fixed goal.

Peace is a journey. That's as close as we can come to saying what it is.

This is what makes retirement such a tricky business. The trick is to keep moving. To stop is to die. Peace is the wife of meaning. Companionship with decency, intercourse with the good.

Divorce is not the ultimate evil in interpersonal relationships, and war is not the ultimate violation of community. The ultimate evil is not caring, or to care only about yourself.

Wrote Presbyterian John Mackay, president emeritus of Princeton Seminary:

> Peace is not the peace of the cemetery . . . Nor is it the peace that came to the Palestinian hillside with

returning spring. The peace which Christ bequeathed to his disciples when he said, "My peace I leave with you," is a dynamic peace whose symbol is the river. Though the waters of the river go cascading over rocky boulders, or swirl through "caverns measureless to man," the river is at peace because its bed is made. So, too, with the People of God, the Community of Christ, the fellowship of love. Its members are at peace in the deepest Christian sense when together they respond to the command of Christ, allowing themselves to become part of God's great scheme of things, emissaries of his grand design.

The priority of peace is one of the dozen gifts of insight youths have to offer. Still, peace has got to be presented and defended as something more than military withdrawal or American contrition.

Peace is an aggressive quality. It sallies forth in the sandals of love. It exalts freedom rather than silence, dialogue rather than distance.

Like happiness, peace can be self-corrupting if it is pursued as an end within itself.

People who live together and have little or nothing to do with each other might be said, in one sense, to live at peace. No guns are fired, no laws are broken, no screams shatter the night. This is not *shalom*. It is sterility.

G. A. Studdert-Kennedy says that there is a "barren ascetic spirituality that has always despised sex and belittled passion, regarding it rather as a danger to than as a means of grace. But this is fatal to the really spiritual life. Flesh and Spirit are in conflict, but it is a creative conflict in which neither must conquer, dominate, nor destroy the other, but locked forever in vital and vivifying combat, seek and be satisfied with no lower peace than the peace of God which passes understanding."

This is close to the heart of what peace is all about—whether we are talking about mental composure, marriage, or international politics. Creative conflict. The cost of being alive, the prerequisite of moving from where we are onto higher ground.

Francois Mauriac, beloved Christian leader whose death occurred in 1970, left us what he called "the secret of the world." Shortly before his death, he said:

> I believe as I did as a child, that life has meaning, a direction, a value; that no suffering is lost, that every tear counts, each drop of blood, that the secret of the world is to be found in St. John's *Deus caritas est*— God is Love.

Peace is definable only in paradox. Paul writes, "Bear one another's burdens, and so fulfil the law of Christ." He follows that statement, five lines later, by saying, "For each man will have to bear his own load." In another place he says, "When I am weak, then I am strong." But the championship for contradiction in the Scriptures must go to these parallel statements: "Peace I leave with you" and "I have not come to bring peace, but a sword."

Jesus offers both. He furnishes a priceless comfort and a lie-awake restiveness—dissatisfaction with ourselves and a saving syllable about contentment.

We must work at the work of peace. William James called athletics one of the moral equivalents of war. The only peace we will ever be able to settle for is peace which has in it the roar of the people and the excitement of the chase.

The seventies present two truths which remain to be proved: First, we need to prove, because the rest of the world does not yet believe us, that our immense American technology is really the friend of peace. Second, that the interracial, intereconomic, intergenerational differences which are pulling us apart as a people are not as strong as the forces and values that contain us in a single comradeship and destiny.

Peace is a journey.

It is closer to work than to sleep. It is more like suffering than serenity.

When we are having dinner on the patio with close friends

and stereo music is being wafted through flickering candlelight, when the children are safe and we have a job to get out of bed for in the morning, we have an innerspring feeling of contentment. Our boats drift lazily along through the mirror-like waters of our own Sea of Tranquility.

Peace is different from quiescence. It is fashioned out of those things that have claimed us and drained us, that have imparted to us a sense of significance.

I don't know where George is today. I hope he is a leader of men somewhere, as he's qualified to be. He has part of the peace answer, because peace requires men of strength and leadership.

Along with George, I'd like to qualify, too, for the favor of the One who said, "Blessed are the peacemakers, for they shall be called sons of God" (Matthew 5:9 RSV).

23
Prayer Creates a New Situation

O God who lives in tenements, goes to segregated schools, is beaten in precincts, is unemployed, help us to know you. . . . O God who is cold in slums in winter, whose playmates are rats, from four-legged ones who live with you to two-legged ones who imprison you, help us to touch you. . . .

—ARCHIE HARGREAVES

Driving up Highway 101 toward San Francisco I am impressed by how the cloud formations overhead are controlled by the mountain ranges below. The coastal mountains, thrust up into the sky, affect the flow of high winds, and those winds rule the clouds.

Another marvel of nature is the relationship between the moon and the tides. As a child, I remember hearing this discussed. I wasn't sure whether it was witchcraft or science. It's science.

Prayer is one name for an active inner life. It describes the interconnection between man's spirit and God's Spirit.

Today the human spirit is in danger. It is under attack. It is floundering. We long for God's Spirit to lead us out of materialistic barrenness into the country called Significance.

What can we make of prayer in a world that knows much about *how* but is unclear about *why*?

One thing is clear: man is not a machine. His eyes may be miniature cameras, his heart a pump, his mind a computer, and his stomach a processing plant. But that is not all of man. Man is essentially spirit.

Though William Faulkner will be long remembered for his novels, he may be even longer remembered because of a remark he made in Stockholm at the time he received a Nobel prize.

> I believe that man will not merely endure; he will prevail. He is immortal, not because he alone among creatures has an inexhaustible voice, but because he has a soul, a spirit capable of compassion and sacrifice and endurance.

Prayer always creates a new situation.

Because it does that, it is a mighty force for renewal. We need to be careful what we say about prayer. It cannot be said that prayer is always good. It can be self-centered, bigoted, and silly. It can be a way of hiding out from duty. It can be a yellow coward. It is not redeemed from those defects merely by adding "in Jesus' name" at the end.

Sometimes it's comical.

A little girl's daddy was a seminary student at Yale. For a long time she thought the Lord's Prayer began: "Our Father who art in New Haven...."

Another child prayed one night, "Good-bye, God, we're moving to Texas!"

But let's go back to work. Prayer *is* work. And prayer creates a new situation.

That's better than saying prayer changes things.

Prayer is not magic. It does not involve the short-circuiting of God's ordered universe. We cannot draw our own little blue circles around what prayer will achieve and what it won't. God doesn't take orders from us. But we distort prayer as a means of grace if we fail to understand that God's principal gift to us in prayer is the gift of the Splendid Spirit.

Prayer to a god who responded to us whimsically would be a spirit of slavery, leading us back into a life of fear. It would be primitive groveling before some monstrous, arms-folded deity! God, heal my leg. God, find me a job. Help me stop drinking.

We have prayed prayers that belong in that category, and we will pray more of them before our lives are over. Sometimes life closes in upon us so ruthlessly we cry these emergency cries, and we're not about to stop and ask whether they are legitimate or not.

But prayer, understood at its best, prayer in the Spirit of Christ, is prayer *for* His Spirit—the prayer that, regardless of what comes, or doesn't come, enables us to fashion the facts into a new part of an unfolding Will.

It is a prayer to love, to trust. Sometimes, to wait.

What is the fresh situation prayer creates? If God doesn't rush in to take our side, do our bidding, or pluck us out of the path of danger, what difference does praying make? Partly this: Prayer renews our humanity. It changes how we feel about ourselves so that we function differently—with less anger, less tension, less concern for what is going to happen to us, and more concern about others.

You can hate somebody intensely, if that's all you do. But

if you are praying for that person at the same time you are holding your negative feelings about him, hate can't stay hate.

If you are full of sorrow and you pray, you slowly begin to deal with yourself on new terms. If you are ill and you pray, your body understands your prayer.

This is not all prayer does. Prayer is not pure autosuggestion because God is involved. God involves Himself with us most helpfully by giving us His Spirit and making us His sons. This doesn't mean we will be exempt from suffering, or death. It does mean we are exempt from becoming embittered human beings, flailing the air, and accusing Him of having awarded us a rotten deal.

This is why the cross stands at the heart of the Christian message. If anything else were there, we might wind up with mixed-up ideas about how God communicates His love.

Prayer is a larger reality than words someone speaks or reads from a printed page. It is inward openness.

> We do not even know how we ought to pray, but through our inarticulate groans the Spirit himself is pleading for us, and God who searches our inmost being knows what the Spirit means. [Romans 8:26 NEB]

In the seventies our prayers are more inarticulate groans than anything else. The war drags on, our economy is shaky, the crime rate grows. The neighborhood policeman has become a pig, the church a deserted village. Dick Gilbert, a young United Presbyterian minister, said on a "Today Show" interview:

> Young people are slipping away from the church in alarming numbers, and I think it is not because they have tried the faith and found it wanting. They have tried the churchmen and found them trying, and the result is a dullness that hangs on the Sunday school walls like mustard gas.

Would I, then, advise that we go off to a corner and pray? It will take more than prayer to lead us out of atheism and chaos. More than prayer. It will take the Jesse Jacksons and the Frank Churches and the Fair Housing Councils. But without prayer, without the strengths and understandings which become part of us when we pray, the dream of a renewed America may die before it is born.

Jesus defined the unpardonable sin as the closed mind, prayer *against* the Spirit. Prayer is the pledge to stay open to God's fresh will. Prayer creates a new situation because it creates a new man: me. Prayer also helps to create a new situation by releasing into the social bloodstream new knowledge of what it means for men to be human. Prayer not only affects the man who prays; it changes others who know we pray. If we know someone else is praying for us, a minimum of two lives are changed.

A child playing on the beach with his shovel and sand bucket alters the curvature of the land—in a tiny, tiny way, of course, but to such an extent that the tides have to take note of it.

To pray is to touch someone else's life. It is to become part of God's presence in a world which requires the fight every inch of the way to stay or else it's losing out to the jungle.

Here the generations split. Much of the Establishment feels that we already enjoy a reasonably human society and dare not see it lost. Those who oppose the Establishment believe that a society which spends half of its tax revenues on armaments is already seriously antihuman.

This is what is under roughest attack at the moment: the human spirit, the nature of man, the intangible "something" that makes us men.

Senator Edmund Muskie was being interviewed on a college campus when a question was put to him about the new morality. His reply included a statement to the effect that at the very least, promiscuous sex is the enemy of the human spirit.

The human spirit has rugged opposition. Paul called it the

forces of darkness. However we name them, they contest our humanity, and we contest them.

War is the largest dehumanizer of all. Its victims include not only those who fall on the battlefield but the rest of us as well, we who develop moral callouses by learning to live with war, to read the casualty figures in a 5:30 newspaper and then to go on and enjoy a big dinner.

The welfare system is another dehumanizer. And the city sometimes crushes out the gentleness in people.

> Blood, guts and war
> Take an aspirin for fast,
> fast, fast relief
> . . . and back to the
> ghetto riot
> . . . or a microphone
> shoved in the face of misery.
>
> Hold on!
> Stay with it.
> You're in the *pattern*.
>
> Find the access ramp
> and swing in with
> the traffic.
> Become part of
> the thundering herd
> of humanity rushing to
> get to the parking lot
> . . . in order to stand in
> line . . . at the theatre,
> at the punch-in clock,
> or at a local drive-in
> (Blink your lights for service).
>
> Everywhere there's a
> pattern, and it's made
> of stop signs,
> go signs,

keep-off-the-grass,
no smoking,
vote!
buy the giant economy size—
and they're all part of
the patterns
like sidewalks of life
that guide us through the day.

But when do you
break out? To where?
To Marlboro country?
Who are you?
How do you establish
your individuality?

Prayer creates a new situation because wherever men are praying they are rebuilding a humanity in which all participate. When a man prays, God joins with him. His Spirit joins with our spirit, and something bright and refreshing is released.

Two years ago a special committee of the faculty at Harvard, including representatives from the colleges of medicine, law, divinity, and others, made a recommendation through the *AMA Journal* that a new definition of death be agreed upon, based upon the total and permanent silence of the brain. Heart stimulators and other supportive devices have made it possible, in recent years, to keep a body operating long after the brain has fallen into a condition of permanent nonfunction. Under carefully regulated circumstances, it was proposed by this group that brain death be considered sufficient grounds to turn off the machines and let a patient enter into the peacefulness of complete physical death.

This may be a good advance. You decide that question as you will. But the recommendation serves to remind us there is more to death than the end of bodily functions.

The only death we need to fear is the death of the spirit— the death of love, the death of hope.

To pray is to affirm life. It is to stay bound up with God's life regardless of how many questions lie upon the ground unanswered.

To pray is to assume that we are neither dead nor alone.
It is to celebrate the heartbeat of the soul.
It is to create a new situation.
It is to inherit the earth, and heaven, too.

24
Four Feet From Death

The distance between the mouth and the heart is less than twelve inches. This is the distance which separates many from God. They have God in their mouths but not in their hearts.

—THOMAS KIRKMAN

At Ghost Ranch in northern New Mexico, several of us went, one August afternoon, on a hike to the top of a large bluff where the land humps up into the sky. These are part of the Sangre de Cristo Mountains, mauve and majestic.

We had taken several children from camp with us and, when we reached the top, we made them stay close to us because of the dangerous cliffs. Resting to get our breath, we huddled in the lemonade shade of a huge boulder together. We gazed out through the thin, clear air upon the infinite pastel landscape.

I was aware, as we crouched there near the edge, that there was still great need to be careful. I found myself thinking:

Here we are, all of us, just four feet from death. Safe, but four feet away—oblivion.

That's the way life is put together.

Disaster, though, is not so much represented by instant death as possibilities unclaimed. God has made us out of fragile material, but like delicate Spode, breakableness is part of beauty.

In the days of Victorian courtesies it was the custom, when referring to future appointments in correspondence, to insert the initials *D.V.*, meaning *Deo volente* or the Lord willing. While that custom has long since disappeared, there remains this reminder of wrongful assumptions in the Letter of James:

> A word with you, you who say, 'Today or tomorrow we will go off to such and such a town and spend a year there trading and making money.' Yet you have no idea what tomorrow will bring. Your life, what is it? You are no more than a mist, seen for a little while and then dispersing. What you ought to say is: 'If it be the Lord's will, we shall live to do this or that.'
> [James 4:13–15 NEB]

It is easy to imagine that life is something we are entitled to, or that it will go on forever, but if we are a patch of fog that appears for a little while, and then disappears, some things ought to be deferred.

We must not forfeit, lest time runs out, the chance to love each other, and let others know about our love.

There is a mournful thought by Thomas Carlyle written in a moment of deep lonesomeness after his wife's death that if he had had her by his side just five minutes longer, he would tell her everything!

A verse by Charles Hanson Towne begins: "Around the corner I have a friend." It describes a man who is too busy to keep up with everything that is going on in the life of his friend who lives "around the corner." One day word comes that Jim died yesterday. Suddenly, the sky is filled with question marks. How important are all the things that have kept me on the run, and Jim and me apart? Now, it's too late.

We may ponder the end of the world, invent images of Earth slipping out of orbit, exploding in flames, or turning finally cold and lifeless, another cold moon against the infinite darkness. Each day *is* that day for someone. Love cannot be postponed.

The first time I heard Robert Browning's "The Grammarian's Funeral," I was a freshman, sitting in college chapel. I never forgot it. In this poem, a great man has died, a scholar, and those who bear his body up the hill with arms rigid, chant a song that it is not sufficient merely to live. One first must learn *how* to live. If one is busy living usefully and enthusiastically, and if love for earth and men and knowledge is part of one's life style, *when* a man dies, or how he dies, is of small consequence. An imaginary conversation with the corpse runs:

> Others mistrust and say, "But time escapes! Live now or never!"
>
> He says, "What's time? Leave Now for dogs and apes! Man has Forever."

Love before it's too late. Love while there's time. And make our gratitude known.

The Bible uses two Greek words for "time." *Chronos* is time understood quantitatively, impersonally. *Kairos* is time understood in terms of the divine purpose. As *kairos,* each moment finds its identity in terms of whether or not God's goals are being reached or thwarted.

The Christian understands *kairos,* and because he believes, God has a plan in mind. Time exists *because* Purpose exists.

We are able to speak about time only because there is regularized movement within the universe. Time is an invention, a device we put together based upon the fact that the earth moves and that living things pass through a cycle of nonexistence, existence, and nonexistence. It needs to be understood as a created gift in the same way that Earth is gift, and breath is gift.

Time is gift as surely as the stars.

Wrote Philip Bailey: "We live in deeds, not years; in thoughts, not breaths; in feelings, not in figures on a dial. We should count time by heart-throbs."

The question is not, Do I have time? but, Am I awake to myself, to the world, and God? If daily we live but four feet from death, we live an equally short distance from life.

To live is to be neither so tied to the past nor so overpowered by thoughts of the "not yet" that we do not recognize how good it is where we are.

We spend weeks preparing for Christmas. Christmas, though, is drab compared to the fun of getting ready.

All life is preparation. That's where the gladness is. The fun of living is journey.

Pick the flowers as you go. Keep your eyes open to wonder. To be alive is to see God in every bush, Christ in every face, the holy in every common thing.

TIME

Make the best possible use of your time. [Colossians 4:5 PHILLIPS]

I have only one thing to do.
    Life's single holy assignment—Luke 10:41–2

I have as much time as anyone.
    All the time in the world—Philippians 4:19

I will set aside moments to be alone.
    Time to be quiet—Matthew 14:23

I will welcome God to my subconscious.
    Clearing the back room—2 Corinthians 5:17

I plan for the future by enjoying today.
   Looking ahead and living now—Luke 14:28–30;
   Matthew 6:34

I do not attempt to do it all.
   No!—Luke 5:15–16

I will make friends with divine interruptions.
   Opportunity in each intrusion—Matthew 9:19–22

I will be courteous of other's time.
   Their time is God's time, too—Luke 6:31

I will live by the secrets of Christian joy.
   The efficiency of gladness—John 15:11

All my time belongs to God.
   The sacrament of every second—1 Corinthians 10:31

CHARLIE SHEDD

VII
TODAY IS THE BEST CHANCE YOU'LL EVER HAVE

25
I'm Telling You Kids for the Last Time!

You have it *now* and that is all your whole life is; now. There is nothing else than now. There is neither yesterday, certainly, nor is there any tomorrow. How old must you be before you know that? There is only now, and if now is only two days, then two days is your life and everything in it will be in proportion. This is how you live a life in two days. And if you will stop complaining and asking for what you never will get, you will have a good life. A good life is not measured by any biblical span.

—Jordan to Maria in
For Whom the Bell Tolls

The title has to be a good one. Whether it's a book, a play, or a song, if the title is right, the writer is halfway home.
Guess Who's Coming to Dinner? A Streetcar Named Desire. The Man with the Golden Arm. Though these titles are now faded by familiarity, they still have spring, a built-in attractiveness that makes us want to find out more.

I wish I could have beaten Sam Keen to the title *Apology for Wonder*. It opens with the following lines dedicated to his father:

And how can I say why?

His life was anchored in the great simplicities of earth:
The touch of the little bodies of children,
The hue of polished stones,
The astringent sun and antiseptic air of the desert,

The elegant geometry of shells and driftwood long bathed in the sea,
The perfume of early blooming lilacs,
The silent testimony of redwood trees,
The refreshment of all that is beautiful and graceful.

And yet there was the resonance of those elusive harmonies at which music hints and for which faith strives.
He lived with a growing ability
To deepen the covenants of friendship,
To admire simplicity and dedication,
To accept limitations and disappointments without resentment,
To forgive the unacceptable and trust the unknown,
To love without grasping,
To be grateful for the gift of life.

In his ambience I learned that it is a good thing to take time to wonder.

Another set of words, spoken by exasperated mothers across the years, has also qualified as the title of a book: *I'm Telling You Kids for the Last Time!*

How many times has the average parent said that? Patience exhausted, sand run out, end of rope, end of line, last call for the dining car, going, going, gone, last chance before you cross the border. This is the *last* time. And I mean it! It's now or never! No family ever grew up or sustained itself six months without the use of that ploy along the way—and more than once. I'm telling you kids for the last time! Pick up your shoes! Turn off the lights! Take those books back to the library; mow the lawn; turn down the record player; go help set the table.

Sometimes it *is* the last time, and failure to comply results in discipline and explosion, penalty or pain. This is what character is made of. There must be some times when it is the last time, when all the options are gone.

In most instances, though, the saying is only threat. It is not the last time. We try again, and when we are not successful, we try some more.

Faith has this ingredient. Love has it. Hope has it. There cannot be any last time if the story of the prodigal is a true statement about God.

Peter asked Jesus how often he had to forgive the one who offended him, who sinned against him, who literally drove him out of his mind. Seven times? That's a lot. "Not seven, Peter. Seventy times seven." We cannot say, "Brother, this is the last time. Shape up or ship out. This is your last go."

The Good News is that we never have that extra try foreclosed. We can always—no matter where we are or how badly life has put us down or what problem has a hammerlock on us—make a new start. We can continue to say, "God, I need a new chance. I ask for it with all my heart and with all the honesty in my blood. I may fail. I certainly have failed in the past, over and over. But I'm asking, nevertheless."

He answers, "There is life even in the asking, and where there is life, there is hope; where there is hunger and thirst, I stand there with food and drink."

Similarly, we never reach a place of final contentment. If someone inquires, "Are you saved?" we reply, "I am saved, I am being saved, and I hope to be saved."

Like manna in the wilderness we research our faith, daily. We cannot do today's work on the food we ate yesterday. As adults we cannot survive on the faith of our childhood. Adultness means endless digging for meaning. If we cannot live on yesterday's food, neither can we live on yesterday's prayers.

There is no last time for faith, hope, or love. These gifts are renewed as regularly as the night is reburnished with the light of the returning sun. But where do we get the spunk and the spirit to try again? When we say to our children that this is their last chance to respond, what we are saying is that we've reached the end of our patience. We're out of gas. Our supply is used up. Sometimes this is the way we feel about everything. We're too tired to try anymore. We're too discouraged, too beaten. Where does one get his second wind?

One place we get it is from each other. That's why loneliness is so tragic. If there's someone beside us there, someone to love us and listen, we can endure anything that life can hand us. Alone we can't hold out long.

Luther, in his essay on Christian freedom, says we are called to be Christs to each other. When we speak, particularly to someone who is hungry for help, our words are Christ's Words. God is alive because we are. A Christian is someone who is open to that possibility. He isn't looking for God to arrive on the scene like a genie, but he is aware of the fact that God may be as close as the person walking by our side.

Another source of second wind is in exposure to the Word. The Bible hasn't lasted two thousand years because it is folk history or because it is filled with stories of staggering occurrences. It has lasted because, in our encounter with it, a living, existential conversation is triggered between God and man.

A man who had made a mess out of his life, who had "done time" in jail, was separated from his family, and was only half-free from an expensive narcotic habit, decided to take a brief holiday visit home. He knew his blunders had been a source of embarrassment to his parents, and he wasn't sure whether he should attempt to go home. He wrote a brief letter. He said that since the train in which he would be returning passed close to his home, he would like for his father and mother to provide a signal if they thought he should return. He asked that they tie a piece of white cloth to a hackberry tree that stood at the back of the house and which could be seen from the train window. If it was visible as his train pulled into the town, he would get off. If he saw no signal, he would interpret the bare tree as an indication that it would be better if he went on through without stopping.

The train rounded the curve, that day, and began to slow down. The man found himself tense with anxiety. To protect himself from too great a hurt, he explained the arrangement to the passenger beside him nearest the window. He asked the fellow passenger if he would look, as the train passed the crossing, to see if there was a tree with some sort of cloth tied to one of the branches.

When he reached the spot, the man closed his eyes. Tears leaked out from beneath his eyelids and dribbled down. The passenger beside him, not fully understanding the meaning of it all, nevertheless grasped his arm as the train reached the point.

"A cloth on a tree? I guess so! There's something tied to every limb!"

"I'm telling you kids for the last time!" Those are only words. Words we use to say how near we are to losing. But there is a God who will not let go—who reasserts His claim, even when we have forfeited ours.

Sometimes strength and hope come through the worship of waiting. "Wait on the Lord: be of good courage, and he shall strengthen thine heart: wait, I say, on the Lord" (Psalms 27:14 KJV). Sometimes our unwillingness to wait is inverted conceit. Sometimes it's evasion or laziness. Sometimes it's the grace of God.

We never know whether our decisions are right. We only know that many of them are not important in the long run. The genuinely important ones have more to do with trust than with theology, more with adoration than with our age.

26
On a Clear Day You Can See Forever

Easter is good news about the universe. It proclaims that the world is not an orphan asylum, not a machine shop, not just a whirling ball, hurled through endless space. It is a home. At its heart is not just something but someone.

—HALFORD LUCCOCK

"On a Clear Day You Can See Forever" may not be one of the greatest songs ever written, but it seems to send the mind on journeys.

Californians appreciate clear days in a special way, because when the air is sparkling—free of fog and smog—this fabulous gold and purple scenery quite overwhelms us. The sight of the blue Pacific, the etched mountain, or palm-fringed skyline chokes us with emotion. Such days cause us to forget others. We bathe in their beauty. We say first to this person, then to the next, "Gosh, have you seen the mountains today!" Our eyes caress the gentle distances. Our bodies fill up with hope. On a clear day you would rather be in southern California than any place else in the world.

Easter, too, is a day for seeing, for distances, for saying *Yes* to life, because God has said *Yes* to us in Jesus Christ.

On the road to Emmaus, Jesus walks along for miles, unidentified, as He talks with two followers about what has been going on in Jerusalem over the weekend. As they walk, though, it begins to grow dark, and it is agreed to stay overnight in Emmaus. "So he went in to stay with them. When he was at table . . . he took the bread and blessed, and broke it, and gave it to them. And their eyes were opened and they recognized him" (Luke 24:29–31 RSV).

It's early morning on the beach. Seven disciples are together. Peter, to get his mind off his sorrow says, "I'm going fishing." The others say, "We'll go along." They get into a boat and push out a little ways. Then, through the morning mist, John sees someone walking on the beach and yells, "Hey—it's Him! It's the Lord!"

"When Simon Peter heard that it was the Lord, he put on his clothes, for he was stripped for work, and sprang into the sea" (John 21:7 RSV). I can see those brown arms of his, thrashing the water, his legs driving hard as soon as he gets near enough to touch bottom.

Clear days. Days when life's murk is blown away, and inside us there is the ripple of transcendence. And poignancy, too, sometimes when the past suddenly floods our feelings with visions of someone we have loved and lost awhile.

There is always, in the midst of talk of life and death, someone's grief that is new, grief that still hurts a lot. For others, though love is undiminished, there is the soft grace of acceptance and Easter Day simply accentuates that love.

Joseph Fort Newton has these words in the opening pages of his autobiography:

> We see the hilltops, but the valleys between are lost to view, except some "glen of gloom," as the Scotch say, where we lost our way and groped in the dark. Some successes we remember, some bad mistakes, some bitter sorrows, some goals achieved, some dreams come true, some faces that never fade, some stupid things said or done in a cruel, careless hour, which we wish we could forget; but the road has become invisible, like a thin thread flung over the hills. Then, suddenly, a little thing, a whiff of perfume, a snatch of a song sung long ago, a face in the street, a chance happening, a voice . . . an old familiar place, brings back troops of memories of people and things we thought we had forgotten: memories that break our heart—and mend it.

One day I was riding along in the car when one of our daughters made a remark. It wasn't what was said at all. It was the mysterious inflection of the voice, and in it I heard my mother's voice stretching twelve years across our last good-bye. We have all had such experiences: a tilt of the head, a facial expression, a laugh, a walk, and someone else's life is relived. The chain of wonder—a whole universe transmitted in the split second of conception.

But what is clear about Easter?

If we were to send a traveling microphone around the congregation on Resurrection Day eliciting ideas about how this mystery can best be explained in the light of modern knowledge, we would get a variety of views. For some, the disappearance of the body and subsequent encounters by the disciples with the risen Christ is enough. For others, the story would be regarded as preposterous, impossible of belief if taken literally. Still others would contend that the truth we meet in Easter is not a risen person but a risen quality of life which has been let loose in the world because Jesus came.

No, that is not all clear. What is clear is that Easter is a hopeful judgment about life. It is a statement which says: Life is a greater reality than death. My version of Easter does not say there is no death. Rather, that though death is real, God is greater than death, and we do not need to be afraid.

The love of God is strange stuff. It contains a quality of helplessness which we see and identify with as Jesus hangs upon the cross. The Crucified doesn't say a few magic words, then zap! rescue Himself. He suffers through a long, humid afternoon—finally dies bleeding, sweating, pale, exhausted, His body racked with pain. In Easter we see another expression of that love—another quality of power. Love cannot be defeated. It rises. Ultimately, it wins. We do not know much about what lies beyond death, but we know God is there, that He is greater than His cross and that because He loves us, we, too, are greater than our dying.

Genesis is a statement about men. It says, through its little cluster of bizarre tales about an apple orchard, a rainstorm, and a tower, that man's biggest problem is himself. Easter is a statement not about man but about God. Also, it is truth couched in a set of stories. If Genesis is to be for us God's living Word of life, we must see *through* the stories, beyond them, see the deeper truth which they contain about man, freedom, and responsibility. We have to look through the Easter stories, too. They must become windows through which we look to see a God who both suffers beside us and leads us to triumph over death and the world.

We are used to saying that *seeing is believing*. Faith puts it the other way around: *Believing is seeing.* A dog trots through the Louvre, but he doesn't *see.* That Jesus is the Christ, come into the world to save sinners, is not a laboratory fact, not something anyone can prove. If Jesus is the Christ for you, it is because you have *seen* Christ-quality in Him.

In the story of Peter and John's hundred-yard dash to the tomb we are told John got there first, that he looked in and *saw* the folded grave clothes lying there. The body of Jesus was gone. The Greek word which is used for John's experience of seeing is *theoreo,* meaning the mere act of vision. When Peter got there, the word used to describe his seeing is *horao* which is to comprehend the *meaning* of what we are looking at.

This is the kind of seeing we try to do within the life of the church. We try to see Christ in each other, see each other's finest human possibilities and needs.

For a long time we looked at the arrangement of American life and thought it looked good. Today we are seeing things we never saw before. We see ecological dilemmas with new urgency. How long, for example, have we provided government-sponsored custodial care for remnant Indian nations, watched their handcraft poverty from a distance, hired them to dress up and dance? But we never entered into an awareness of their longing to achieve the dignity and independence most of us take for granted.

A lot of our seeing is *theoreo*—optical vision, but little more. Maybe that has to be. But if it's the final sum of our seeing, then we are dead. We were really made for *horao*—for involvement in the meanings that are all around us, meanings that lie half hidden within what our tiny eye cameras are taking pictures of.

Don't you see? we say to each other. Often we don't, on the first go-around. We have to keep trying.

There are, thank God, *some* moments of sudden seeing—Easter moments.

If in the resurrection story we see God still at work trying to restore the broken cities and societies of men, calling each of us daily out of death into life—to the deeper life of seeing, caring, and giving—then what happened to the disciples will happen to us, too. The resurrection will have been proved in the one way it has been—the only way it can be proved.

Forever is a long time. Time without limit. Love has no limits. Neither does God.

Our family decided to spend an afternoon at the beach. There, my daughter Mary Scott and I went to work on some sand sculpture. Since everyone makes sand castles, we thought we'd try something new. We hit on the idea of making a model of our dog, Albert. But after we'd finished, "Albert" looked more like a donkey than a dog. So we chose to make use of serendipity and said, "You are not a dog. You are a donkey." Then we made Jesus on his back; added sand children waving sand palm branches on either side of him, and finally capped off our work by carving just above our Palm Sunday scene the word *Hosanna*. We left it there—our witness that Christians had ventured that way.

Our lives are like that. We set out to make one thing and God does something else with it. What look like crowns sometimes turn into crosses, and our crosses have strange ways of turning into crowns.

A Good Friday speaker told the story of the founding of the John Tracy Hearing Clinic for children. He recounted a conversation Mrs. Spencer Tracy had with the doctor in the days just following the realization that her beloved child, who had been welcomed with such joy, could not, and according to the physician, probably never would be able to hear. Said the doctor, "Mrs. Tracy, you are an especially blessed woman. Helping John is bound to guarantee you a most interesting life."

The tides wash away the sand. Yet, something stays, something remains, something endures. The human spirit is a precious commodity. We drag it through the dirt, neglect it, let it become contaminated by hate and fear and jealousy and greed. But it goes on. Love goes on. Faith goes on.

Whether John Tracy can hear or not winds up as not the real question at all.

Easter is the gift of life because it is the gift of seeing, the power to hope, the will to believe that beyond death is God and life. Our lives are mortgaged to both of these truths.

Of Jesus, Liston Pope has written in *Preaching the Resurrection:*

> In every age, Christ lives and works and dies and rises. He is born again and again. In our lives, shabby stables though they are, he may be cradled. He grows again, and those in whom he grows come to wisdom and stature. He comes again to our temples and confounds the learned and the wise. He comes with healing and forgiveness; the blind see, and the lame walk, and we being evil know how to give good gifts. He comes with imperious demands, so that we are never easy in our comfort, never adequate in our love. He will not let us be, this ruler of eternity who struggles with the souls of every age.

On a clear day you can see forever!

27
When We're Crying
We Know We're Not Dead

The closest I could come to a contemporary definition of sin would be to call it inaction in the face of knowledge.

—CARL RADOV

The Sunday after Easter is tinted with irony. After the most exhilarating day of the year, "Low Sunday" is characterized by letdown feelings and a sermon by the Assistant Pastor.

Where do our thoughts turn when Easter is over—when the new dresses are back in the closet and the pink and blue hard-boiled eggs have been converted into egg salad sandwiches?

Sam Shoemaker of Pittsburgh once wrote about young men entering the ministry. After a few years of ecclesiastical storekeeping, he said, they tend to become glum and dispassionate, both about themselves and their message. He asked, "Where goes the glow?"

The day men greet each other by saying "Christ is risen!" divides the Christian year into two parts. From the first expectant sounds of Advent in early December to the Easter Alleluias, the mind of the church is on what God has done for man.

Advent opens by rehearsing long centuries of waiting for the Messiah. Habakkuk cries: "O Lord, how long shall I cry for help, and thou wilt not hear?" Isaiah promises his exiled countrymen that God's power to help is restricted only by the requirements of love.

Then Jesus is born, and the universe shouts.

There follow several weeks during which the church retraces His earthly ministry. Jesus becomes God's man—God in man—God the teacher, physician, the friend of sinners, a son to His mother, a brother to His brothers, a problem to the Sanhedrin. A man of candor, humor, questions, and long dusty walks along narrow roads.

The forty days of Lent arrive, emblematic of days spent in the wilderness. Then the hard highway to Calvary.

With the Easter triumph, the curtain falls upon Act I.

Act II deals with man's response. Because God has come, man's life is different. It is mortgaged to a new truth. God has acted. Now, man must act. He must become *part* of new truth. He is called to be an agent of reconciliation. Knowledge of the Man-for-others becomes the inspiration of his life lived for others.

The tears which mark the route to Easter have a value, but only if they put us in touch with a deeper awareness of ourselves.

Carlyle Marney taught me their real meaning in *The Crucible of Redemption:*

> How difficult it is to keep Easter without slushy sentiment. Better to let it go, some say, than to spill over it with slush—or is it? A friend said that if it were not for the Junior Chamber of Commerce fighting over who would sponsor the Sunrise Service, it wouldn't be Easter in Jackson this year. But we keep it here. We spend an eight-day week at it here. We put over a thousand man hours into it here. We print books and worship programs about it. We quit work and assemble. We bring gladly the singers and the preparation and the lilies and the symbols. We sit intently. We listen. We visit our neighbor and sister churches and we worship. We cluster around the grave and cross a week—we mean business here with our weeping—but starkly, too, we hear him say, "Weep not for me."
>
> No annual weeping in some sanctuary does any good. No clustering up in little bands of women or men, no lingering in the pews to cry, no loitering, over a prayer-band diversion. "Weep not for me"— don't hand this seasonal splurge of tears and lament, this fever of reading devotional treatises. No memorial floral piece dropped tearfully on a mound of sorrows annually is either expiation for, or commitment to, anything that matters. No sermon tasting. No daily pilgrimage will do it. No Lenten diet. No theological binge. No embalming sentiment. No assembly of women at the well or women at a wedding or women at Lazarus' grave or at Christ's grave

can make any difference to him or to us. For he, on his way through, for us and for our salvation says, "Weep not for me." But there is a proper weeping.

"Weep for yourselves and for your children." And what could that mean except this: if you are going to cry, cry about the same things he cried about. Turn your eyes upon the object of his weeping. Identify with the reason he was sacrificed. If you weep, weep for that which makes God weep. Join that lonely cry in Samuel Miller's libretto for the oratorio "What Is Man?" Here the great God Almighty sees his creature turning away from him, and God sends up and out that heartbroken cry, "Adam!"

Weep that we always did reverse things. We always did foul the cup; profane the holy. Weep even for the animals, says Father Zossima in *The Brothers Karamazov,* who do not soil the earth as we men do.

So, we weep for lost dimensions, over swamps we and our fathers and grandfathers created; we weep for a culture we dare not abandon because we know nothing created by us would replace it. Weep, if you wish, that you cannot redeem yourself. Weep that we wear his name and not his power. Weep for politicians, weep for white racists. Weep for Negro hate and neighborhood scandal and crime and ignorance. Weep for slavery magnified with gadgets. And weep for Mount Zion, shrouded there in the mist, but always in our reach. Weep for Viet Nam and South Mississippi and Washington Heights in Charlotte. Weep for Watts, Detroit, Newark, and old Brooklyn. Weep for our history and our future. And more —weep for the children. For always in the Scriptures, since Jeremiah at least, the children of the desolate, the abandoned wife's children, have been more numerous than the children of the marriage. There is a proper weeping. He turns us toward it.

There is plenty to cry about in our present civilization. The beauty of tears is that when we are crying, we know we're not dead. Tears may represent the noise of our worn-out illusions, hitting the floor, shattering into a million pieces.

If our tears are to wash away the dirt and open the way to something promising and new, they will have to be tears that enable us to catch a vision of the more authentic self we can become.

We will not achieve greatness of spirit by looking for it in far places. It is at hand, reaching toward us through the everyday opportunities to be forgiving, to speak some word or perform some act that will help someone else to believe in himself.

Easter means it is time to move out of the season of crying. If we enter into the wounds of the world and make them our own, the dove of peace will fly into the world on the wings of a new and natural humanity.

28
Open Your Heart to Spring

Is it not by his high superfluousness we know
Our God?
For to equal a need
Is natural, animal, mineral: But to fling
Rainbows over the rain
And beauty over the moon, and secret rainbows
On the domes of deep sea-shells,
And make the necessary embrace of breeding
Beautiful also as fire,
Not even the weeds to multiply without blossom

> Nor the birds without music:
> There is the great humaneness at the heart of things,
> The extravagant kindness. . . .
>
> —ROBINSON JEFFERS

It was April. That, perhaps, is enough to say. On a westward drive across the country I had arrived by late afternoon in the southwest corner of Kentucky where the Mississippi crossing is at a remnant of a town called Columbus. Unfamiliar with the surroundings, I studied the skyline for a hint of an overhead bridge. Instead, the highway led directly down into the water without a sign of a ferry slip. I reached for the map to see where I had wandered off the route.

In that split second, lowering sunlight fell upon the river in front of me, turning it into a golden fire. Lifting my eyes, I caught in the distance a glimpse of a comical tug, towing an oversized raft, coming to take me across.

With the help of two loading planks, a dollar bill, and a soft, five o'clock wind, I helped myself that afternoon to a satisfying drink from a Mark Twain cup of spring.

Paul Tillich described what happens to us in such uncontrived ecstasies: "Joy," he wrote, "is born out of union with reality itself."

Though there is a country-mile distance between Biblical faith and pantheistic intoxication, there is, nevertheless, a special version of insight that comes to us through encounter with creation itself. Especially with spring. Harriet Moore felt it:

> Larks are sparkin' down in the meadow,
> Bees are squeezin', cozy as can be,
> Bugs are huggin', robins are throbbin',
> The woodpecker's neckin' in the old oak tree.
>
> See the crocus work his hocus pocus
> Suddenly the earth is bright and gay . . .

Winter is necessary, I suppose. It means nitrogen for the ground, business for ski resorts, the enchantment of Christmas Eve. It also has a way of graying us within. It means slushy streets, four-way cold tablets, icy rain, empty swimming pools, cancelled meetings. The earth is brown and sterile. Overcoated citizens hurry along the street without seeing each other.

Then comes a day when, through an open door, there is the smell of the gulf. On dogwoods and maples, miniature green signals appear. Suddenly we feel that exhilarating brightness at the end of April's resurrection wand.

> Bobolinks are winkin', turtle doves are lovin'
> The whole world seems to say
> Hey, there! Open your heart to Spring!

What do such poetic experiences have to do with the tough issues of human meaning we have been working away at? There is more to the Christian position than sunny talk about bobolinks and buttercups.

Yes, more.

The vernal equinox of the spirit arrives when we learn that Earth's "extravagant kindness" is a hint that God is kind, too, and that He discloses this to us most forcefully in Jesus. The carpenter's Son is the divine expression of God who surprises us with joy, who opens our hearts to rebirth, to forgivability, and the springtime of faith.

Around the beginning of the second century a man described this process in a single sentence. It read: "If we walk in the light as he himself [God] is in the light, then we share together a common life, and we are being cleansed from every sin by the blood of Jesus his Son" (1 John 1:7 NEB). This statement says, with simple impressiveness, that God is love, and that when we respond to that love, our lives are as eloquent as the universe itself.

> The human heart can go to the lengths of God.
> Dark and cold as we may be, but this

Is no winter now. The frozen misery
Of centuries breaks, cracks, begins to move.
The thunder is the thunder of the floes,
The thaw, the flood, the upstart Spring.

CHRISTOPHER FRY

Christians are called to look on the hope-filled side of every human situation. It is risky to make that a statement in the midst of the new pessimism. A folk song philosophizes, "You can't get to Heaven on roller skates!" You can't get there on soft sentiment either. But to face life affirmatively is not to lapse into rose-colored delusion any more than it is irreverent to capitalize on moments of humor and lightness when sorrow is heavy in the air.

As we mature in knowledge of our world and the people in it, we are involved in a natural drift toward life's dirtier side. We come onstage as starry-eyed innocents who see the planet as a spread-out Disneyland. We are capable of being fascinated even by a fistful of dandelions. Wars are gallant moments when brave men march down the streets to stirring band music in the defense of liberty. Then age begins to stain us with its disenchantments. We start getting acquainted with life's compromise and stink.

In Somerset Maugham's story "Rain," a woman with a calcified soul has the final word:

"You men! You filthy, dirty pigs! You're all the same, all of you. Pigs! Pigs!"

We may never hit that low, but we do grow coarser and less tender the more we grasp of the predicament of man. Original sin may be double-talk in our teens, but gradually its meaning becomes believable and plain. As it takes muscle to turn a ship against a heavy crosscurrent, it also takes strength of faith to resist today's flood tides of despair.

The invitation of this book has not been to travel in the poor light of some theory about inevitable progress. Nor in the candle flame of self-hypnosis. It is to walk in the brightness of God's purpose made known to us through our life in spiritual community. It is to adopt Melvin Wheatley's philosophy:

> To have no more physical dangers to brave, no more intellectual questions to answer; no more moral and ethical and spiritual peaks to climb—that is the most barren plight of all. For a man's reach does exceed his grasp, and that is what a heaven is for. It is a place in which we reject any whimpering wish to crawl back into that static state of tranquil irresponsibility and instead of that, march gladly forth into this vale of soul-making, affirming this old world of ours as:
> a hazardous place in which to be safe, but
> a glorious place in which to be brave;
> a confusing place in which to be sure, but
> a fascinating place in which to be curious:
> a devil of a place in which to harvest a soul, but
> God's own kind of place in which to grow one.

Football coaches in August enjoy drawing these overcast sketches. If an athletic director predicts his team will win the Conference, he is tabbed a novice. If he admits with reluctance that it may win one game, he is treated with far more respect, and suspicion. Similarly, it requires no effort to imagine all kinds of hydrogen horrors waiting for us around the corner of the future. It is right that we should give these latest threats the clear-headed treatment they deserve. But it is error to believe that our whole future is in our own exclusive and frail custody or that God is unconcerned with the outcome or unable to do anything about it. God is not dead. Nor asleep. Winter will not last forever. As Harriet Moore wrote:

> Bid goodbye to the snow.
> Say hello
>   to springtime's rosy glow.

The People of God have learned the hard lessons of hope in the wilderness. They have been verified in the miracle of Easter. They are rekindled by His living Spirit—breathed into the desperate moments of each man's time.

We should trust tomorrow and cherish a strong vision of its possibilities. Jesus never made glib denials of the problems faith faces. Instead He answered, "Now I will ask you a question," redirecting our attention to the rebuttals of goodness. Consider the lilies of the field. Ponder the miracle of friendship. Study the gifts of prayer, thought, sound, color, and sight. Think of those in whom you have found the harmonies of speechless communion. Look at the silver permanence of stars, the blue power of the sea, the pink miracle of a baby's thumb.

The love of God is not forensically proved, any more than is the beauty of April. These are personal options. We are free to write our definitions of what they mean.

The Christian life is not a life that ducks the facts. It is life that borrows light from the Light that lightens every man's coming into the world.

> Come on—take a deep breath and sing
> And everyone can hear you
> Tell the whole world—it's Spring!
> And good luck!

When God made *you*, He knew what He was doing.

FIRST BAPTIST CHURCH LIBRARY
TOMBALL, TEXAS